Rajvi is a student of Iyengar Yoga, having studied directly under Guruji B.K.S. Iyengar, and Geeta and Prashant Iyengar for many decades. She has travelled to many countries to teach yoga in the tradition of B.K.S. Iyengar, to experience first-hand how Guruji B.K.S. Iyengar, through this subject of yoga, has unified the world, cutting across all barriers of language, geo-political ideologies, socio-economic conditions and cultural differences. She is the founder-editor of the magazine *Yoga Rahasya*, which has been published for the last twenty-six years. She is currently involved in modern scientific research on Iyengar Yoga. She is a reproductive biologist by training and profession.

IMAGINE IF

STORIES OF ORDINARY PEOPLE WITH EXTRAORDINARY GRIT

RAJVI H. MEHTA

First published by Westland Publications Private Limited in 2021

1st Floor, A Block, East Wing, Plot No. 40, SP Infocity, Dr MGR Salai, Perungudi, Kandanchavadi, Chennai 600096

Westland and the Westland logo are the trademarks of Westland Publications Private Limited, or its affiliates.

ISBN: 9788194879022

Typeset by SÜRYA, New Delhi

Dedicated to my parents,
Mrs Bhanumati and Mr Hasmukh Mehta

And my guru yogacharya,
B.K.S. Iyengar

Contents

Suffering: A Choice?

> *Nature provides the means to adjust to the rhythm of life with all the turmoil of day-to-day pressures and environment.*
>
> –B.K.S. Iyengar

The Bhagvad Gita states, 'Birth, disease, old age and death are part and parcel of life.' Once we have taken the human form, we have to face all these issues and nobody in this world is free from this. If we are lucky we may be saved from these issues in our childhood and youth, but they will show their face at some point in time. It's a fact of life.

Life is not always happy. Pain and suffering are entwined in everyone's journey. What is interesting is how we define suffering. The dictionary defines it as a state of undergoing pain, distress and hardship. And here is the catch. Everyone's perception of what pain, distress and hardship are is so relative.

Let's take the example of hardship. It is defined as 'severe' suffering and deprivation. Again, what is 'severe' is also so relative. Imagine yourself as someone who has been brought up with all the possible comforts in life. As a college student, your parents provided you with an air-conditioned car and a driver. One day, the driver does not turn up and there is nobody to drive you to college. The most likely reaction of somebody who is accustomed to being driven around would be, 'How do I get anywhere? I have no car.' Having to commute by a taxi or a bus—something that one has never done before—is seen as a 'hardship'.

On the other hand, there are millions of people who travel daily in the jam-packed local trains of Mumbai. The trains are so crowded at rush hour that if a person shifts a bit, they will disturb five other people. When their station approaches and they have to move towards the door, they have to twist and turn their bodies, lift their arms over their heads, so they can make their way out. They travel in this manner every day and have therefore accepted this situation. There are commuters who are lucky enough to find a seat, albeit squashed! And they remain in this state sometimes for over two hours, chatting, singing, reading or even preparing vegetables for the dinner they have to make when they get home. A person used to being chauffeur-driven everywhere may consider this as hardship, but for most of the commuters, it's just part of everyday life, and they would rather sing and chat than moan and groan. The feeling of hardship and suffering is all about how one perceives things.

This example shows us that people are capable of handling extreme situations, but it is up to the individual human mind as to how it perceives these situations.

The result of hardship is the experience of suffering and pain, which are expressed both in the physical and in the emotional form. Even these experiences are relative. Imagine somebody who is hale and hearty. She is approaching middle age and has been coughing for weeks without any relief despite over-the-counter medicines or home remedies. She now needs to undergo an X-ray to identify the cause of the problem. She is petrified by the sight of a hospital and the thought has already generated much more anxiety than the physical pain caused by the coughing did. She wants to will away the problem; she imagines that it has become better in the last two days and she does not need to go to the hospital any more. Her mind has already started playing games: could it be tuberculosis, could it be fibrosis, could it be cancer, could it be COPD, which has no cure and is one of the world's leading causes of death? Her Dr Google has already given her many options for the diagnosis and it is now for her to decide which one to pick. Her physical pain is now superseded by the emotional pain.

Take another example of a woman who has been suffering from back pain for a while. Her endurance level is quite high and she manages her day-to-day life presuming that her pain is due to the large shopping bags she lifted a few days ago and the long journey she had to make after that. She assumes that, with time, it will disappear. The pain is an irritant but it has not led to any suffering. A friend then advises that she should see a doctor rather than live with the pain. A series of investigations follow, and the diagnosis is spinal cancer. Till the diagnosis, the woman was managing her life well, but the diagnosis leads to a sudden deterioration of her physical condition. The state of her mind started reflecting on the body. Her mental pain led to her physical pain.

And then we hear the stories of some sages from India. Ramakrishna Paramahansa from Kolkata and Ramana Maharishi from Tiruvanamalli. They 'suffered' from cancer. They experienced all the symptoms that go with the disease. But for reasons known only to them, they did not appear to be 'suffering'. They were yogis, they were enlightened beings.

These three examples clearly show us that pain and suffering are subject to how one looks at them, how one accepts them and how one handles them. It is all the play of perception.

The consequences of how we perceive our suffering alter our behaviour as well as that of others towards us.

In the case of these sages, people thronged to be with them, be in their presence and listen to their words of wisdom. They were suffering, but being in their presence helped people move away from their own suffering.

On the other hand, if a person constantly complains about their problems, they are initially met with sympathy and guidance, but at some point, people will probably start avoiding them. People have their own problems, and they do not want to be burdened by somebody else's constant complaining.

Over the last few decades, I've met people who, according to me, had extra-ordinary problems; but they did not make these problems larger than life—they always let them remain a 'part' of life.

Imagine losing everything in an earthquake, literally everything: family, papers and property. How does one cope with that?

Imagine losing your vision in an accident at the age of twenty-two. When a colourful life suddenly becomes dark. When one has to relearn everything.

Imagine you are an outdoor person with a love for the mountains, and you lose both your legs in a landmine when you are in your twenties. Now, forget climbing mountains, climbing onto a bed from a wheelchair is an ordeal.

Imagine what life would be like if all your means of communication slowly shut down? When your vision, hearing and speech are gone. Would you stick to a corner of your home, barely existing?

Imagine somebody losing control over their emotions and behaviour and committing a dastardly crime. A crime which deserves the worst of punishments? What happens in one of the most secure prisons in the world?

Imagine leading a life full of interruptions—interruptions caused by cancer and its treatments. And handling not just one but five cancers, the first at the age of twenty-two.

These are real people and real stories, stories full of grit and determination, where the people did not see their problems as an end, but as a new beginning. And the common thread between these stories is that they are all about practitioners of Iyengar Yoga.

As Guruji Iyengar said, 'Yoga teaches us to cure what need not be endured and endure what cannot be cured.'

I hope these stories inspire readers as much as they inspired me.

Cancer or Common Cold: It Is a Part of Life

> *Yoga teaches us to cure what need not be endured and endure what cannot be cured.*
>
> –B.K.S. Iyengar

Israel, a small country with a population of around eight million, always seems to make it to the headlines, whether for its politics or for its history, culture and science or simply for the zeal of its people. My experience with Israelis was minimal until we met a few students at our institute, Ramamani Iyengar Memorial Yoga Institute (RIMYI), in Pune.

For many years, India did not have any diplomatic relationship with Israel. Our passports were marked 'Not valid for South Africa and Israel'. So when the doors of Israel opened for us, I was curious to visit this intriguing country.

But when my brother Birjoo was invited to teach in Israel in early 2000 in the midst of the war in the Middle East, we were petrified. The newspapers kept writing about the shelling, and we wondered why he had to go; the Israelis could come to India to learn. They wrote back saying that all was well and they would take good care of him. We did not doubt their hospitality and concern, but what could they do against the uncertainties of the war? They managed to convince us that there were problems only in isolated pockets. But from afar, it seemed to us that the whole nation was affected. After all the assurances, he did travel and, of course, came back safely.

A year later, the Israeli family that had hosted my brother decided to come to India for a holiday—a couple and their two teenage daughters. They stayed in the touristy area of south Mumbai and decided to walk to the Gateway of India, before joining friends for lunch. This was the first visit for their daughters. The onslaught of crowds, colours, smells and sounds in the large city of Mumbai frightened the young girls, who were from a small village. Their senses were stressed. One of them lost her hair clip and turned cranky. To give them a break from the intense assault on their senses, the family decided to go back to the hotel, unaware that exactly ten minutes later there would be a bomb blast at the Gateway of India leaving fifty-four dead and nearly two hundred and fifty injured. The Israelis had never been so close to a blast in their own country! I had perceived that there was a high chance of being caught between missiles and blasts in Israel, while they had never been as close to one as they were in Mumbai. This is the irony of perceptions and nature!

When I received my first invitation to teach yoga in Israel, I could not resist. I was curious to visit this Promised Land—a land always submerged in controversies and immersed in history. Jerusalem, where three religions of the world 'meet', is a city which cannot be described with words. You need time to understand its complexities.

It was during this visit that I met a person who changed my perspective on life and living. I do not know whether it was the Israeli grit or it was growing up with the stories of a mother who had survived the Holocaust, but this person, Shirly, was not 'normal'.

My first encounter with Shirly was in Tel Aviv at an Iyengar Yoga workshop which was being taught by Birjoo and me. One of us was to teach the class and the other provide assistance to the students who needed it. All were regular practitioners of Iyengar Yoga. As in most cases, this workshop too was well organised. There were local teachers too to help students who had health issues or other concerns. However, everybody was a part of the class and nobody behaved casually. That was the discipline inculcated in the students.

So it was very surprising for me to see a young woman walking across the hall quite aimlessly, not even making an attempt to follow the class. She did not seem involved with the teachings at all. As this was my first class in Israel, I walked up to her and asked her why she was not participating in the class and if she was unwell. If she was unwell, I would take her to the side and help her practice to recover from whatever she was suffering from. She looked quite well, but I did not want to be rude. Her answer was simple. Guruji had given her a special sequence of asanas to practice and she would be doing that.

I found her refusal to listen to the teacher rude but I did not want to make a scene in my very first class. So I politely asked her about her problem. She said, 'Oh, I have cancer,' and smiled. Her expression seemed to imply that she was joking, but why would anybody even want to joke about such a dreadful disease? Then she continued to stroll around the classroom, went out, came back again and sat on the floor in Upavishtha Konasana—the class was doing something else—and then intently listened to the teacher. It was a little annoying, as the teacher was not lecturing but giving instructions about doing specific asanas which the students were expected to follow.

I decided that it was best to leave her alone for the moment and not get disturbed by her. While I did ignore her for the rest of the session, I kept wondering whether I had heard her correctly. Didn't she say she had cancer?

But the way she was behaving, it seemed she was at ease with her disease.

Certain words have the capacity to generate a sense of fear. One such word is cancer. The moment it is uttered, it sends shivers down our spine and our heart sinks. Of course, later we come to terms with it and move on, but the immediate reaction is always shock and fear.

Take the example of a person who has had back pain for a while. This dull pain comes and goes, so he does not give much importance to it. It must have been due to over-exercising in the gym or lifting a heavy bag, he thinks. As the pain continues for too long, he decides to visit a doctor who advises him to undergo certain tests.

The test results say cancer of the bones. The moment he hears the word, his mind sinks. Should he have visited the doctor earlier? Why him? He doesn't smoke or drink or have any 'bad' habits. How much time does he have? How serious is it? Is it treatable? How expensive is the treatment? Will he recover? Which stage is it?

A barrage of questions bombard the brain, not necessarily in a logical sequence. The back pain is no longer a mild irritant which interfered with work. In fact, now work is secondary and interfering with the treatment of the back pain—not only for the patient but also for close family members. This disease, unlike many others, generates such a scare that it seems to take happiness out of our life.

My mind came back to the present. I was sure that I had not heard her correctly; she did have an accent. But I did not want to disturb her or, for that matter, disturb myself, by asking her again. To be honest, she did look like the kind who would not get disturbed, but I would surely be disturbing the rest of the class by talking to her. So I left her alone for the moment.

During the break, I went back to her and asked again what was wrong with her. She said, 'Nothing is wrong with me. I had taken some treatment many years ago, and am getting the side effects now.' This conversation was taking me nowhere. First, this woman had told me she has cancer and therefore cannot participate in the class, then she says she is experiencing a side effect of a treatment she had received many years ago. I had heard of the side effects of cancer therapy, but she seemed to be telling me that her cancer itself was a side effect of some other therapy.

Later, I asked some senior Israeli teachers in the group about her. They told me that her name was Shirly. She had visited Guruji in Pune many times and they let her follow whatever Guruji had advised her for her cancer. However, she was always very keen to attend sessions by any visiting teacher and do whatever possible. Oh. She did have cancer! I was genuinely taken aback.

My irritation with her transformed into curiosity. I wanted to know more about her, her disease, her yoga practices and how she coped with everything.

After the initial workshop in Tel Aviv, there was another workshop in a kibbutz, only for the teachers. It was residential, so the classes were longer and we interacted much more with the participants. Shirly was present here too. Was she also a teacher? I learnt later that she taught cancer patients in the Tel HaShomer as well as Ichilov hospitals in Tel Aviv.

Here, too, her behaviour was similar, except that she was more intent on listening to the teachers. In the middle of one afternoon session, she informed me that she was going out to make an urgent call to the hospital. 'I need to find out whether my test results say cancer or not.' My heart was possibly beating faster than hers. How could she be so calm in the midst of such a life-threatening disease whose treatment seemed as bad as the disease itself. I would probably be more stressed before the results of an ordinary blood test for a fever.

When she came back, I asked her whether all was okay and she shrugged and said, 'Yes. It has come back.' And then went back to participate in the class.

Was she referring to her cancer? Did she have a relapse? I did not have the heart to ask her. I was also feeling a little guilty about the way that I had doubted her earlier. After some time, I garnered some courage and went up to her. 'I am so sorry about the diagnosis. Would you be going back to Tel Aviv for treatment? Is there anything that I can do to help you?' In reality, I had no clue as to how to handle that situation.

She just smiled and said, 'I knew what the test result would be. I had told the doctors, but they do not believe the patient, they believe a piece of paper. So I had to do the tests for them. So now they can do their treatment.' And she went back to class.

She knew exactly what was happening to her. Her sensitivity to her own body was much more than any diagnostic test, and here, I was so insensitive to her. I was glad that I had not been rude to her and all my thoughts about her behaviour had not ventured out as speech. But my conscience questioned my insensitivity. I definitely needed to meet this 'character'. She was beyond the ordinary.

A year later, she was in Pune at the institute so I asked her if I could interview her about how she had fought the disease. She laughed out loud. 'You want me to talk about my fight against cancer. I don't fight. Fighting and war take away energy. Why would I waste energy? I need the energy to live life and not fight. I don't understand why people want to fight. I just look the disease in the eye and accept it and live with it.'

I was taken aback. 'Fighting' was such a common term used in relation to this disease—I had heard about foods that fight cancer, people that fight cancer. And here she had said, 'Fighting takes away energy. I need the energy to live.' How did nobody think of that before? That explained her approach and the calmness with which she had accepted her disease as another fact of life. There was so much to learn from this statement. We argue and fight with people with different views and ideologies, but what good is that? We only lose our energy. Why waste our energy on what we don't like? Why not just 'accept'? Even in our daily life, differences that arise between couples or families or members of the society, out of a simple mismatch of behaviours and habits, break them apart. If we just accept others as they are—with their thoughts, habits, behaviours and views—the world would be a much better place. And we would all be smiling because we don't fight.

For her, it was a simple statement—a fact of life.

Then she continued, 'That's why it is important for me that people understand. People who have cancer find it hard to think like that. It's like a part of your body that you don't like, but at some stage you have to accept it. In the same way, I understood that I must accept my cancer for what it is, and so I do not make war on it.' Shirly's words were profound. We fight against what we don't like. We waste our energy doing that. The loss is ours. Why can't we just accept this and rather use our energy to work around it and for something we like?

People give lectures on yoga, on philosophy, but here was a person living philosophically under what appeared to me as adverse conditions. She was living the yoga sutras, which state, 'maitri karuna mudita upekshanam, sukha duhkha punya apunya …' Accept things that are not conducive to you and move on …

She then formally introduced herself. 'I am Shirly Ecker. As you can see, I am an albino and I have nystagmus—involuntary eye movement. And yes, also—I almost forgot—cancer. Well, actually, a few types of cancer. It started with Hodgkin's but then there were others.' I was stunned. I could not imagine the plight of anybody who had five relapses of cancer, with her first cancer at the age of twenty-two. At an age when people live to turn their myriad dreams into reality—dreams of a career, a family, seeing the world, living life to the fullest—how would it feel to be suddenly woken up by the reality of cancer?

I definitely wanted to know more about her and her story of where she got this strength and ability to look diseases like cancer in the eye and not fear it, fight it or feel depressed about it.

Shirly had had a normal childhood—as normal as it could be with both parents being Holocaust survivors. Her mother was saved from a concentration camp by a Polish family, while her father, a physics professor, had worked in the Israeli air force. Both her parents did yoga. One day, while doing her Sarvangasana, she felt something was not right in her throat. It was an odd feeling. So she approached a doctor. He examined her and told her that there was nothing wrong with her. She insisted that she felt something different when she did her Sarvangasana and her breathing was altered. Her doctor had a simple answer. 'Then don't do it.' Moulding the body in that position seemed to him more abnormal than the complaint Shirly had come with. This was more than twenty-five years ago when the medical fraternity did not know about yoga, let alone appreciate its effect on human life. What could Shirly do? She continued her life, ignoring the doctor's suggestion of stopping Sarvangasana.

Six months later, the 'real' symptoms were evident. She started losing weight and had night sweats. With these symptoms she went back to the doctor who could now diagnose her condition as Hodgkin's lymphoma, a tumour which needed to be treated with chemo and radiotherapy.

It was interesting that six months before the 'known' symptoms of cancer surfaced, Shirly had sensed the symptoms herself during her yoga practice.

The diagnosis did not worry Shirly much. She had known that something was not right six months earlier and at least now it had been diagnosed. The treatment started with chemotherapy and radiotherapy. Her physicist father was not too keen on radiotherapy, worried that the therapy itself could lead to cancer in the future. But the doctors were confident and they had no evidence which substantiated his fears. Generally, in case of cancer, patients are considered 'cured' if they remain in complete remission for at least five years. The definition of cure differed between the doctor and the father. The doctor had his way and Shirly was given radiotherapy. She endured the related ups and downs with full support from her parents and two sisters, hoping that it was just an uncomfortable patch in her life that hindered her graduation in social work.

Unlike most people, Shirly wasn't worried or even afraid of cancer. Why could she not befriend it instead? Little did she realise then that cancer would become her very good friend and keep coming back again and again. Today, Shirly has spent more years of her life with cancer than without. She has had five relapses of different cancers in a span of thirty years—Hodgkin's, Merkel cell or skin cancer and, most recently, breast cancer.

Anybody else in her place, including me, would have been shattered. But if you happen to meet Shirly, you would be made to believe that she was suffering from nothing more than a common cold. It comes and goes, and you don't give it so much importance. You do what needs to be done but definitely don't overreact. All this is easier said than done. We can give 'profound' advice to not worry or be bothered about the cancer since there are therapies and treatment. But not many would be able to handle these conditions with so much ease. Shirly said it all in one statement: 'Cancer is a part of life; don't make it bigger than life.'

It was so true. Whenever there is a problem, we get so absorbed in it that it puts our life on hold. Everything else that was important a day before becomes redundant. But Shirly taught me with her own example that life goes on, we accept whatever comes, without putting our life on hold. We continue doing whatever we possibly can. So often, overwhelmed by problems, we forget that they are just a part of life; we give them so much importance that they take away our life from us. The problem becomes the focus of everything. Shirly indeed had a real problem. She attended to it with whatever therapy was possible but did not get bogged down. How many of us have that ability to not get bogged down by our problem? During the very recent lockdown all over India, to help maintain social distancing and prevent the spread of the COVID-19 virus, I was surprised at the major problems that most of the residents in my building faced. These young professionals put umpteen posts on our chat groups complaining about the time and effort that went into household chores. Surprisingly, none of them commented on the pleasures of being home with the family, saving commute time or not having to worry about their kids in the crèche. Our mind has this tendency to focus on the problems alone.

Consider our history lessons. We learnt about the three battles of Panipat, the two world wars and the events that led to them. We learn about these events because they changed the world. But I wonder why we also don't learn in detail about all the good times in between. Why not learn about life during the times of peace and tranquillity?

Why don't we give as much importance to what is positive around us? Maybe because we want to prevent becoming complacent when things are going well, we train ourselves to stay apprehensive so that we can develop the capacity to handle any eventuality. But what if we could be prepared for all eventualities and yet see the good things around us?

Shirly was teaching me a big lesson on how to accept problems, even if it is cancer, as a part of life and not make it bigger than life itself. Initially, I had felt that she was in denial, not accepting her situation and therefore not getting affected. Denial is unhealthy because at some point of time we will have to face the reality, and then it would appear graver and more difficult to accept. But in her case, it was very clear that she just saw things differently. Her focus was on the beauty of life—even when she was in the hospital.

Most of us, as patients or caregivers, don't even notice the décor in hospitals as we focus only on our diagnosis and treatment. Not Shirly. During her stay in the hospital, she took amazing photographs within the premises. They were like works of art. She even had an exhibition of her photographs taken in the oncology unit of Sheba Hospital—an exhibition of photographs from a hospital, photographs which had nothing to do with medicine. She quipped, 'You can live even if you have cancer, and not just live, but live big-time. You can get excited about things—even during the treatments, you can find a reason to say "Wow!" I always find a wow. I found the places with the most amazing sunsets and sunrises.' She said that it is up to each individual what they wish to latch on to: the sickness or the non-sickness.

When we have a disease, we are usually not sick all of the time. There are bouts of sickness and bouts of remission. Why not focus instead on the bouts of non-sickness? These were soothing words. When there is a problem of any sort, we get bogged down, but if we could focus on the gaps, life could give us solutions. That was Shirly. She did not look at the disease but at the non-disease. It was all about perception.

But as much as we focus on the non-sickness, it is only natural that our mind wonders about the future, both of the disease and of life.

Shirly had a simple answer for that too. 'What is the point of worrying? Yes, science has some knowledge and therefore gives you a prognosis. But it does not have 100 per cent knowledge. If it did, then there would be nothing to worry about. But since it does not, what is the point of worrying about it?' She equated cancer with the common cold. Cancer or common cold, science has no answers, she said. And she did not just say it. She meant it.

In the intermediate phases of life, when Shirly was not in the midst of treatment or follow-up, she spent a lot of time travelling across the world, whether to Europe, Japan or

India. India was always on the list and she would make at least one trip a year to RIMYI or travel around the country which had not been where she was born, but which had given her life with yoga and our dear Guruji.

After recovering from her first cancer, Hodgkin's lymphoma, Shirly had visited India with a group of Israeli students. She was now well and without any health issues, so she decided to join the general classes. It was her first class at the institute and with her friends, she entered the hall. After the invocation, while she was on the second asana, an assistant teacher tapped her shoulder and asked her to shift from the main class to the back of the hall where people with medical conditions were being helped.

Shirly was surprised. She had not spoken to anybody about her medical condition, which in any case she thought had been cured. She was about to argue, but before she spoke, she figured out that the teacher had been sent by Guruji, who had noticed 'something' about her. Guruji said that she should not attend the general classes but the medical classes, and that he would personally guide her.

How had Guruji figured out her history by looking at her back from the end of the hall? She had been cured. The disease had not left behind any visible physical scars. Shirly had always practised yoga, respected yoga and the man behind it. But this was unanticipated. How had Guruji known? But that was Guruji, an epitome of insight who could see your problems, present and future, much before anybody else could. After that, Shirly was totally under his care; she followed and practised yoga as per his advice and the receptivity of her own body.

This is when I told Shirly that, during all our interactions, she had never really mentioned much about her yoga practice. I asked whether she did yoga every day. Her answer was curt. 'What is there to say about it? Do you tell people that you brush your teeth every day? It is understood.' This statement got etched in my mind. How true it was! I have always found it amusing when people keep saying 'I do this diligently every day', 'I am a very generous person', 'I am very sincere', 'I love my work', or 'I love my yoga practice'. If we need to talk about any activity or any trait of ours, then it is not intrinsic to us, it is not part of us but separate from us.

Later, Shirly shared with me many photographs of her yoga practice in the hospital bed while she was undergoing chemotherapy. She had to lie in the hospital bed with an intravenous drip through which the chemo drugs were being administered. Imagine lying there for a few hours, doing nothing. Unpleasant thoughts and doubts would creep in. Sliding into depression is easy; the treatment itself could add to it. The heart sinks, even if you are a Shirly, strong and unfocussed on the illness. How could she uplift the emotions? The answer was simple—by propping up the emotional centre, the region of the heart. As there was a lot of time in hand, she used it fruitfully and allowed her creativity to surface. Picking up the disposed empty rectangular boxes of the vials of injections, she placed them on the bed, rolled up her socks tightly, and she had a 'prop' to prop up her chest, the emotional centre. Her breath became smoother and her mind quieter.

Besides the commonly known side effects of the treatment—nausea and loss of hair—there were other less obvious side effects. Shirly felt as though the extremities of her body 'were melting away'. Without any personal experience, I understood it to mean numbness in the fingers, hands, toes and feet, a sense of non-existence. But when Shirly gave a talk to cancer patients in a support group, all of them started nodding at this statement, as if she had given words to their experience.

She had a solution for that as well. She demonstrated certain modifications of asanas like Upavishtha Konasana and Supta Padangushthasana. She had her belt, and the pole on which the bottle of the IV drip was hung became an innovative support for her feet.

I was quite surprised that the doctors and nurses permitted her to do what she did. I do not know whether they were confident of her experience with the disease or overwhelmed by her or simply lacked the patience or stamina to argue with her. Or possibly, they did not have anything better to give her.

I feel it was a combination of all these. Once, when she was admitted to the hospital a day before for the presurgery work-up, she suddenly felt like having a party. Call it stubbornness or determination, if she wanted it, she did it. A party was planned that evening. The location was the waiting lounge in the outpatient department, as usually nobody was around late in the evening. A few of her friends came in with food and music and they danced through the evening.

If she had told this to me earlier, I would have thought that she had imagined it. But after getting to know her, I knew that anything was possible. And the photographs of her happily dancing were the proof. I do not believe that none of the hospital staff noticed this scene. I am sure somebody did, but maybe they kept quiet and did not report it to the authorities. Happiness and joy in a cancer ward is a rarity, and who does not want happiness!

Once, when she was to be operated on for a growth on her para-thyroid gland, on her way to the operation theatre, she suddenly realised that for a few days she would not be able to do her favourite Sarvangasana. So she decided to do it immediately. She requested her doctor's permission to delay the procedure by a few minutes so that she could do her Sarvangasana. And Shirly being what she was always carried a bolster on her hospital visits, like others carry a purse or a wallet. Once she was in Sarvangasana, her mind was pacified and the subconscious nervousness quietened. She was ready for the surgery.

I do not know what to call her behaviour. Certainly not impulsive, because she didn't do things randomly without thinking about them. She had a clear pattern. Accepting her disease, she let the medical professionals do what they felt was right and good for her, while she focussed on the non-sickness, the beauty of life. It was natural for her to do things that gave her joy—whether a dance or a party or Sarvangasana. She was literally living in the moment, like great philosophers tell us to do. That was what made her accept the disease and its treatment with ease.

She found that, besides the asanas, the environment played a big role too. The hospital bed was not the best place to enable her to step back from the disease. In most situations, she managed to divert her mind while practising her asanas during chemotherapy, but sometimes she needed more support from the environment. On one such day, she carried her bottle with the drug to the children's ward, which had a more pleasant environment, with colourful toys and paintings. There she lay with her bottle of IV in an empty children's room with her hands in Sanmukhi mudra, calming her eyes—the windows to the 'active' brain.

Many of the things that Shirly ended up doing in the hospital were revolutionary, or should I say rebellious. But what harm can such behaviour do if one rebels against cancer? It may cause inconvenience, but if it helps the patient, then isn't it worth the inconvenience?

Shirly had spent a lot of time in the Tel HaShomer and Ichilov hospitals and she took me on a tour of the cancer ward of Ichilov. It was not a tour that I wanted to go on, but I did not have the heart to tell her. So she walked around like a professional, telling me matter-of-factly the state of each patient in the rooms that we passed through. This one would go home soon; this one will not be there more than a week. She said it all so calmly—these were just facts for her. I wanted to move faster, as I could not handle it further.

Some of these patients smiled at Shirly. They were her students. She taught yoga to the lung cancer patients at the hospital. It is one of the deadliest cancers with a poor prognosis. So the doctors, patients and caregivers were always a little stressed and anxious. How do we ease such stress? Guruji and Geetaji always educated us on how tension and anxiety reflect as hardness in the abdomen—no wonder the idiom for anxiety is 'butterflies in the stomach'. Relaxing the abdomen makes it easier to control the anxiety. One of the easiest ways to 'quieten' the abdomen is to lie down straight but keep the legs bent at the knees, with the back of the knees and the lower part of the thighs supported. The hospital did not have the yoga props, but Guruji had always innovated the props from household items. So Shirly managed to use water bottles to support the legs, and the expression on the face of each patient changed. These were the patients who were greeting Shirly from their rooms with a smile.

Some people may be sceptical about such a simple solution. But they fail to realise that this simple solution has come after years of sadhana by Guruji, to study the interconnections and interactions among the different parts of the body. It requires a genius to make things simple.

Life is uncertain. Not even the best astrologers or doctors know what will happen tomorrow. I have heard about cases where people passed away immediately after getting perfectly normal health reports. I knew a friend who visited a cardiologist for a routine check-up, returned home with a sigh of relief because all was well, and passed away from a massive heart attack just two hours later. However, the uncertainty weighs much more with cancer. When cancer strikes, the reality of death also hits us. As Shirly says, 'There is no time.' So why waste it? Do what you want when the going is good. These words reminded me of Sant Kabir's lyrical doha, 'Do today what you intended to do tomorrow, and do now what you wanted to do today.'

I remember Guruji always living in the now. Never ever did he postpone anything. I remember the time when his assistant Kumar was on leave. Kumar helped Guruji respond to the dozens of letters he received every day. This was before the era of the internet. So Guruji would dictate his response and Kumar would type it and send off the mail. When Kumar did not come for a few days, Guruji himself replied to all the letters. He was about to write an address on an envelope when one of his old students walked into the library. He was shocked at what Guruji was doing and took over the task, but for Guruji it was no big deal. It was a big lesson but often difficult to implement. Shirly's attitude reminded me of Guruji's yogic life.

Life is often equated with a journey. A journey where there are milestones to touch and goalposts to reach. A journey where there are responsibilities and desires to be fulfilled—desires for ourselves, of those around us and sometimes of society. How do we decide whether the journey has been successful? We consider it successful when we reach our destination and fulfil the purpose of the journey. For a musician travelling for a concert, the journey does not end on reaching the concert hall but after an enthralling performance. For a researcher travelling to share his research at a conference, the journey is successful if the paper is well accepted. The journey of a mountaineer on an expedition is successful on summiting the peak. But what if the journey does not lead to the desired outcome? What if the musician's presentation is not appreciated, the researcher's findings are criticised or the climber is unable to summit? Is the journey unsuccessful? After the initial disappointment, we console ourselves or are consoled by family, friends, teachers and peers that there is some learning in failure too. Failures are the stepping stones to success. Thus we start preparing for the next attempt and then the next attempt and then the next, and life moves on.

But what happens when major interruptions show up in this journey and shatter our plans and timelines—like with cancer therapy? Most of the time, we want to make up for the time that has been 'wasted'. Shirly told me that was a big mistake. 'You may leave the hospital but the side effects do come home with you. You should just accept that that time was meant for therapy. You may keep thinking that you have to make up for the time lost, that your colleagues have moved ahead on a project that you had started. But so what? Accept it and start where you had left off—otherwise all that you get is unhappiness about missing out.' This reminded me of Lord Krishna's words: we have a right to our actions but not the fruits of the actions. We should enjoy the journey and not bother about the outcome. That was exactly what Shirly was doing. She made it a point to enjoy and seek neutrality even in the most trying times.

It has been over fifteen years that I have known Shirly, and in this time, I remember her having three relapses and undergoing the full range of treatment. Shirly has not seen life in continuity as most of us have, but rather, a life full of long interruptions. She has accepted those breaks, not thinking of them as interruptions but as times to pause. For her, life is not a race or competition, so she enjoys the journey. I do not know where she got her grit. She attributes it to her genes and her two gurus—her yoga guru B.K.S. Iyengar and her doctor. As she says, 'The art of living is to know what to observe and what to enhance.'

If Shirly has no complaints about life and can live happily even in these apparently adverse conditions, I wonder whether any of us has a right to complain about life. All we need to do is develop the perspective to accept, focus on areas that are not problematic and see any adversity as a new beginning, a new way to see life.

Freedom in Captivity

Freedom with discipline is true freedom.

–B.K.S. Iyengar

I may not be totally wrong if I were to say that all of us have made errors and mistakes, cheated, lied or even broken the law at some point of time in our lives, especially if we have lived a few decades. Many of you may not accept this statement—you may say, 'Please don't generalise! I am a law-abiding citizen. I have never cheated in my life.' But perhaps it was an action that was not intentional but inadvertent. Maybe we did something wrong for a good cause. Maybe, it was a white lie—an untruth that does less harm than the truth.

As college students, many of us photocopied chapters or even entire books instead of buying them. I remember doing that myself, and I admit that at that point of time I had no idea that it was 'wrong', that I was violating any law. Books were meant to educate. Did the source from where the 'book' was procured matter? I still have the photocopy of my favourite immunology textbook with me. Even today, students photocopy entire books or download PDFs and circulate them among fellow students. In fact, a renowned publishing house recently filed a case against a shop offering photocopying services near a university in Delhi.

Why do students do these 'illegal' activities? Well, most do not even realise that photocopying books is unethical—their seniors have done it; their teachers know about it and nobody has ever stopped them. Moreover, some books are prohibitively priced and the college library does not have sufficient copies for every student to take home. Later, when I got involved in editing and publishing books, I realised my mistake—but did not really repent it. I did not, however, repeat those acts of felony!

Given this background, I was stunned to receive an email from a woman in Manchester in the UK, asking me permission to photocopy one of our publications, *Yoga in Action: A Preliminary Course* written by Dr Geeta S. Iyengar, Guruji's eldest daughter and a guru in her own right. Wow! Somebody was seeking permission to make ten photocopies of our book! But instead of appreciating her honesty, I started acting high and mighty. That is the folly of the human mind. When somebody gives us some importance, we start behaving as if we are among the most important people in this world, little realising that we are 'important' only for that specific moment, specific act or specific position. Ideally, the 'real' you should not be affected. But as we grow and attain degrees, position and honour, we tend to get carried away and start associating ourselves with these. But that is the story of a common human being. Learned, self-realised souls remain unaffected.

So, with this misplaced sense of authority, I sent a barrage of questions and interrogative emails. 'You do not need to photocopy the book. You can buy it from so and so.' The woman wrote back saying that she was aware of where the book was available, since she herself had bought a copy. And, as mentioned in her first email, she was willing to pay for the ten photocopies. How could I trust her? The fact that she wanted to photocopy and not buy the book meant something was not right. What if she made more copies? It was a simple black and white book. What could her intention be? Would she make a business of it? Strangely, when I and many others had done the same thing, even if out of ignorance, I had not questioned my motives and actions. But here I was doubting a lady who had 'honestly' asked for permission! Even if she had made those copies, how in the world would I have known?

She replied that she taught in a prison and the authorities did not allow this book as it was spiral-bound. I was surprised again. Why should the binding matter? In fact, since this was a manual, it had been spiral-bound to prevent damage due to exhaustive use.

Finally, I checked her credentials with the Iyengar Yoga Association of UK. My doubts were put to rest when they told me that Sharon Dawn Taylor was indeed a certified teacher of Iyengar Yoga. She belonged to my fraternity and I had full trust in her now!

How our mind plays games! We justify our wrong actions and judge those of others as unethical! Our doubt of a stranger's words becomes blind trust when they turn out to belong to our fraternity or community or even nationality—as if 'our' people could do no wrong!

I looked at her request differently now. Of course, she could photocopy the book. But now I was more curious as to why a spiral-bound book would be restricted for yoga students in a prison. Then, I learnt that Sharon taught Iyengar Yoga to convicted sex offenders in a special isolation area in a high-security prison in Hull near Manchester. They were considered vulnerable as they were at a high risk of being attacked by other inmates. She wanted to provide two reference books to these students—*Preliminary Course* by Geeta S. Iyengar and the classic *Light on Yoga* by Guruji B.K.S. Iyengar. Sharon had not thought that procuring ten books would be such a challenge. All she needed was to get some funds to buy them. She had requested the Iyengar Yoga Association of UK as well as Paul Walker of Yogamatters, himself an Iyengar Yoga student, and both these organisations were generous enough to sponsor copies of both these books. After all, Guruji said, 'Giving does not impoverish and withholding does not enrich.' Sharon took the copies of *Preliminary Course* to the prison warden for permission, which she did not get. The warden believed that the inmates could remove the thin metal spiral and injure somebody with it. Then Sharon offered to remove it and tie up the pages with thread. Even that was not allowed. These inmates were convicts; they could harm themselves or somebody else. One had to be cautious. Although they were supportive of Sharon teaching yoga, they could not take a chance and permit these books.

When all her attempts failed, Sharon decided to write to the publisher and the mail landed in my inbox. While she had a tough time convincing the jail authorities that her students would not harm themselves or others, she had a tougher time convincing me that her students could harm themselves with the spiral spine. What irony! However, her persistence influenced me and I talked with Geetaji, the author, and the permission was granted.

As the photocopies entered the walls of the Hull prison, my mind did too. My thoughts wandered towards crime and punishment, criminals and prisons—something that had never been on my radar before. My encounters with prisons were through novels, movies and the crowds, mainly of women, waiting with lunch boxes outside Arthur Road Jail in Mumbai—quite similar to young women standing with lunch boxes outside schools. This comparison may sound caustic, but in truth, both groups were waiting to provide the comfort of homemade food to their loved ones who were within the walls. The walls of the school were to protect the children from the vagaries of the outside world, while the walls of the prison were to protect the outside world from the vagaries of the minds of the inmates. I suddenly became sympathetic towards the inmates of the prison. My mind moved into the prison and then into their minds.

Life in a prison must be quite stressful. Enclosed in a world far away from reality, feared or disdained by society, some convicts may repent and wish to make amends, while some may feel dejected about the unjustness of their punishment. Aristotle said, 'Man is a social animal. Society is something that precedes the individual.' Being cut away from society must surely be traumatic.

Yoga helps people in traumatic conditions. Guruji said, 'Yoga teaches us to cure what need not be endured and endure what cannot be cured.' My respect for Sharon increased; she was helping prison inmates withstand the trauma of isolation.

What makes people commit crimes? I am no criminologist or psychologist, but as an observer of life,

I think that crimes may be of two types: premeditated or impulsive, caused by loss of emotional balance. Most crimes have their origins in the shada-ripu—the six emotional enemies—kama (lust), krodha (anger), lobha (greed), moha (infatuation), mada (pride) and matsarya (jealousy). Road rage is a bout of anger fuelled perhaps by the jealousy of somebody overtaking one. Road rage incidents involving influential people are a result of a combination of pride and anger. Crimes of greed can be anything from pickpocketing to bank heists. Most teen crimes, including heinous acid attacks, are a combination of infatuation, anger and jealousy.

Do these 'criminals' repent once their emotions settle? Or do they justify their crimes? Would they now gain some 'freedom' from shada-ripu? Or will they re-enter the criminal mindset?

All humans have a conscience. When we do something wrong, our 'conscience' pricks us—even if the 'wrong' has not been noticed by anyone. The first prick is strong, but when we stop paying it any heed, it doesn't jab at us anymore. Guruji often spoke about the different layers of health: health of the body—of the muscles and bones, the organs and organ systems; health of the mind, emotions and intelligence; moral health; social health and finally health of the conscience. Children give least importance to their physical health, but their conscience is healthy. They cannot let go of a wrong deed as easily as they forget a fall or a fight. If the parents and the teachers are approachable, they immediately inform them and get rid of their guilt. Children may make many mistakes, but any wrong they do intentionally bothers them. Innately, their concern for the health of their conscience is much more than their concern for the health of their bones, muscles or organs. On the other hand, adults are much more concerned about their physical health—how often do we talk about the problems with our knees and spine rather than those with our conscience! Possibly, in the journey of life, our conscience gets buried deep and we become insensitive to small deviations from the truth.

If one commits a crime, irrespective of the intent, one needs to be punished for one's misdeed, as well as to deter others. But can punishment really discourage all people from becoming criminals? Inside a prison, whether a convict turns into a better human being or into a hardened criminal depends on whether their conscience resurfaces or gets buried deeper. And if criminal tendencies are indeed governed by neurological activities, as MRIs have shown us, what is needed is a transformation of the criminal.

Guruji said, 'Yoga does not change the way a person sees things; it transforms the person who sees.' My respect for Sharon Dawn Taylor increased further. She was indeed working on transforming criminal minds.

I was curious to see what she did in the restricted environment of the prisons and thought I would visit the

Hull prison during one of my trips to the UK to teach at the national convention. I thought that all I had to do was inform Sharon—I still had traces of my sense of superiority—and then accompany her when she went there to teach.

But getting into the prison was not as easy as I had thought. I had to send an email with my biodata and a copy of my passport and get a series of permissions, which took longer than the documents required for my visit to the UK. But finally, I was allowed entry into this prison.

At last, the day arrived, and we—my brother, my fellow teachers from the UK and I—drove down to Hull. There was quietness all around. The high brick walls of this old structure were intimidating. Inside, burly security officers sat behind a glass window; they were more daunting than the walls. I smiled and handed over our permissions. Our 'host' Sharon was already in and they called her from wherever she was. We waited, looking about. There were cupboards full of keys, thousands of them, all neatly arranged. I had never seen even one-tenth that number in my life.

Soon, Sharon appeared on the other side of the glass wall. She was not permitted to come out and meet us. Having arrived early, we waited and joked amongst ourselves that we were the rare people who were trying so hard to get into a prison, possibly harder than the people trying to get out! Finally, our turn came, and an officer accompanied us, carrying a bunch of keys. He opened a large metal door and we walked through a corridor with metal walls—twelve to fifteen feet high—with grills and barbed wire at the top. At the other end was another door, which was opened with a different key, and once again we walked through a long corridor with metal walls and grills. At the end was another door. Finally, I understood what 'security' meant.

I fail to recollect how many such doors and corridors we walked through. I did not have a smartphone on me to count my steps but I am sure I completed my daily quota of walking. While walking through those grilled corridors, we could see a few buildings—the gymnasium, hospital, kitchen and the room for the guard dogs.

During the walk, the security officer turned into our guide, and told us that these days there was more focus on the rehabilitation of prisoners than on punishment. This prison had one employee for every two inmates—a high ratio, possibly needed to rehabilitate as well as control some of them, in case their neurons were activated again.

We climbed up stairs to reach the yoga hall where the students and Sharon were present. There were guards all around. We were asked to sit in a corner and watch the class in progress. We were all senior Iyengar Yoga teachers and we were told very clearly not to touch any student or adjust their posture. I refer to them as students of yoga rather than inmates or prisoners or convicts or criminals because Guruji taught us to not discriminate between students based on their religion, vocation or socio-economic background. That was true here too.

It looked like any other beginners' yoga class. The students organised themselves and followed Sharon's instructions diligently. Once in a while, we added a few tips and they listened to each word, missing no instruction. This was unlike in our general classes where we often need to repeat instructions since students occasionally have difficulty following them or get distracted. I realised that these men were so used to being instructed, that they could follow the yoga instructions with ease.

Any word of appreciation for their practice brought an expression of satisfaction and happiness to their faces. If they answered a question correctly and it was appreciated, we could sense their pleasure. As unnerving and formidable as the walk to this yoga session had been, there was a sense of calmness and comfort in the class, although I was amidst repeat sexual offenders. Neither their gazes nor their expressions were indicative of their crimes. They were on their best behaviour, as though they felt that their performance was an assessment of their teacher in front of her seniors—although of course we had no such intentions.

I later learnt from Sharon that this was the way they normally behaved; it was not put on for us. Having labelled them as 'offenders' in my mind, I had sceptically attributed their good behaviour to our presence or the effect of yoga. But they were human beings despite their crimes. Their conscience had perhaps gone deep into a cave. If the rehabilitation could bring it out, then the human being in them would be expressed.

After the class, they gathered their props—mainly blankets, mats and belts—and the guards counted them. The security guards showed us how even mats could be torn into strips and turned into a potential threat. But would the practice of yoga nullify or reduce the tendencies?

After the class, I had an opportunity to interact with the men. They had questions too. One of them had borrowed *Light on Yoga* from the prison library and was wondering where we practised yoga in India. I was a little surprised at the question. Then, he added, 'I am told that it is always sunny in India and *Light on Yoga* mentions that we should not practise in the sun.' It was an innocent question from a naïve young boy!

One of the older men said that he practised in his cell and he wished there was more space. He shared his tiny cell with another inmate and it was so small, if one of them got up, the other had to sit on the bed. With not enough space for the two of them, they practised yoga on their beds or even did simple asanas like Pashchima Namaskar. He added that whatever they did was giving him relief from the back pain he had acquired due to living in a constrained space.

Another man expressed that he always looked forward to the classes. 'We feel nice and quiet after the class, so it must be doing something to us and our minds.' Sharon was teaching them yogasanas from the photocopies of the *Preliminary Course*. They too referred to those time and again. While 'scholars' debate that asanas are for the body and the other aspects of ashtanga yoga, like dharana and dhyana, are for the mind, these practitioners realised that what they did with their bodies calmed their minds too. Guruji often said, 'How do you know where the body ends and the mind begins? The body and mind are so closely integrated.'

Being a strong proponent of yoga, I wanted to believe that it was indeed transforming these inmates. But, at the same time, my rational mind could not accept fully that yoga had a big role to play.

I got my answer after a few minutes. Once our interaction with the students was over, they were taken away by the officers. We were to now walk back through the corridors, which had been empty when we had come in. Now, many of the other inmates were waiting in a queue to return to their cells after their 'activity' time. The lights were not very bright. And as we walked down the stairs, we heard loud boos, jeers and lewd remarks. There was so much noise, although the officers were trying to quieten the inmates. It was frightening. I kept my eyes on the steps, not having the courage to look up at their faces. I could not gather whether this was their normal behaviour or whether it was triggered by the rare sight of women and visitors. All I could conclude was that yoga must have made a difference to the students we had met even if they were only acting well behaved in our presence—at least they had wanted to appear that way before their guests.

My curiosity increased, especially with regard to the early phases. How were the inmates introduced and motivated to practice yoga? I learned that Sharon's mother used to teach in a prison. When Sharon was a little older, she volunteered to teach maths at an open prison for women. Later, she offered them therapy in the form of acupressure. Being a practitioner and teacher of Iyengar Yoga, she then felt that she should introduce this transformative practice to them too, and approached the authorities. They welcomed the suggestion. They had also heard about the calming effects of yoga but had not been able to find a yoga teacher who was willing to teach in a prison. It involved too many security hassles and restrictions on teaching methods. Of course, the teacher needed to have the experience of handling such people also.

The first thing that Sharon had learnt was not to refer to their crimes. Many of the prisoners already experienced remorse and guilt. So she never asked them or the officials about the reasons for their imprisonment. Guruji said, 'Externally, treat your students as students, but internally treat them as a godsend. You are learning by helping them. They make you understand, and you must give them respect.'

Respect was the keyword—this was something that the inmates had lost in the eyes of common people. Even after serving their term, they would have to learn to live without respect, for with the needle of suspicion always ready to point at them, their entire life may not be sufficient to regain dignity and respect.

Sharon knew she had to treat them as students of yoga independent of their social history. It took time for them to make eye contact with their teacher. They constantly looked at the floor—whether out of shame or out of habitual obedience. So Sharon read out these words by Guruji and said that mutual respect was necessary not just between student and teacher but between each of them.

Although she did not ask about their crimes, some of the inmates still revealed their reasons for imprisonment. They wanted to check whether she lived by what she had quoted. Would she still respect them or was 'respect' just sweet talk? Sharon earned their respect by giving them respect.

Respect has to be earned, not commanded or demanded. The demand for respect arises out of one's ego and often has disastrous results—like ragging in educational institutions, where seniors demand respect from their juniors out of a misplaced sense of superiority. If we can teach everyone to respect all fellow beings from childhood, the world would surely be a better place. We should teach not merely through words but through our behaviour and actions as well. Parents may give a long discourse to their children on the importance of respecting fellow human beings, but if they themselves behave badly towards their domestic help, then their children will imitate that behaviour, and not follow what they have been told to do.

Likewise, Sharon's normal behaviour with them and lack of curiosity about their past gave her students confidence, and after a few classes, their gaze shifted from the floor to her eyes.

But as much as she respected the students, she had to be cautious. They were in prison for a reason and were undergoing rehabilitation. Even if they were well-behaved, she had no way of knowing whether or not something could trigger violent behaviour. Take the example of drug addicts. The real test for drug addicts who have been institutionalised, medicated and counselled is whether their desire is triggered when they are offered drugs and nobody is watching them. Transformation takes time. So Sharon had to ensure that there were no triggers—whether humiliation or anger or sexual desires. She could not touch any of the male students or even wear her usual yoga wear of t-shirt and shorts or tights. She wore a loose outfit, which the authorities called the 'Widow Twankey outfit', referring to an amusing character in the pantomime, Aladdin.

In such an institution, the students were so used to listening to commands that even if they were asked to do something painful, they took it as punishment and obeyed. It was imperative for Sharon to ensure that the students did not see yoga as a punishment too. So none of the students were forced to attend the yoga class. They were given a choice between any physical activity and yoga. Initially, they did not complain of pain even if they did an incorrect movement during their asana practice, and Sharon had to ensure that they informed her of the pain and could differentiate between healthy pain and unhealthy pain. She would continuously have a dialogue and observe their faces to fathom what they were feeling. This also enhanced their own sensitivity.

In a prison, space in all forms, physical and emotional, is lacking. Many of the inmates came from socio-economic backgrounds where they themselves had been victims of physical abuse. Their personal space had been violated and they had subsequently violated somebody else's. In an open prison, they could move around and form groups for their activities, but in a closed prison, such mingling was not allowed. They were vulnerable and one had to be careful that they did not harm themselves or others. Although Sharon had permission to physically adjust the women in the open prison, she never did so without asking their permission before each adjustment. So they respected her for respecting the personal space of their bodies.

In such institutions, people also lose their right to make choices, even simple ones like what to eat, when to eat, what they like to do or not do. Perhaps rightly so, because it is their own wrong decisions, or decisions taken under someone's influence, that landed them in prison. Sharon had to inculcate in them the faculty of making small choices and thinking about the consequences of their choices and decisions. In the yoga class, they were asked to decide whether they wanted to do a Setu Bandha Sarvangasana or an Ardha Halasana. Or if they preferred doing Supta Baddha Konasana with their feet against the wall or with a support for the back. These choices may seem trivial to those of us who are living in a free world. But this way, the prisoners learnt to listen to their own selves—how do I feel when I do Setu Bandha Sarvangasana compared to when I do Ardha Halasana? What does my body and mind need now? They start feeling more involved. They feel their space even within the confines of the prison.

The students themselves had categorised the asanas on the basis of space efficiency. They used the photocopies of *Preliminary Course* as a guide for their practice inside their cells. The security guards confided that they saw inmates practising in their cells—one of them was even trying hard to attain balance in Ardha Chandrasana!

'Freedom with discipline is true freedom,' said Guruji. Freedom is not to behave as per our whims and fancies. It is to make discriminative choices. We have freedom; we are not in prison; but we need to ask ourselves if we have true freedom. Are we being inadvertently dictated by our shada-ripu of lust, anger, infatuation, pride, jealousy and greed? Are they stubbing out our rational thoughts and making us act in manners which are not reflective of a thinking human being? We need to get our conscience to surface to such an extent that it, and not the shada-ripu, dictates what we do. If the practice of yoga helps in giving freedom to those in captivity, it can surely free us from our own chains of desires and bondage.

Look Ma—No Legs

The body is the institution, the teacher is within.

–B.K.S. Iyengar

Prenatal yoga classes are getting quite popular these days. Many obstetricians recommend yoga to pregnant women from the second trimester onwards, as they believe it will facilitate the healthy growth of the foetus and ease the delivery. However, as yoga teachers, we recommend that women start yoga even before conception. Of course, we teach them even if they come while pregnant, but we find it amusing as well as annoying when they want to join the medical or therapy classes where we teach people to tackle their specific health problems or diseases. Pregnancy can cause dis-ease, but it surely is not a disease.

Morning sickness is a common discomfort in the first trimester—so common, in fact, that it became a popular trope for old Hindi films to depict pregnancy; within the simplistic narrative of the films, whether this morning sickness became a joyful occasion or a tension-packed one depended on whether the woman was married.

The exact cause of morning sickness is not known. It is thought to be due to the human chorionic gonadotropin (hCG) hormone, which maintains the pregnancy. Some would say that it is the Supreme's way of ensuring the mother-to-be eats right, rests and slows down her life. Women have always been looking for tips to overcome this discomfort. But what if the solution leads to disaster? That is exactly what happened in the 1960s.

In a world recovering from the agonies of war, people were increasingly troubled by sleeplessness and anxiety. The use of sedatives and tranquillisers was picking up. One such drug that came into the market was thalidomide. Trials on rats had shown that it was a safe drug even in pregnancy—even higher doses had not indicated any side effects in the rats. People began taking this pill for a restful night's sleep. And an obstetrician soon noticed a pleasant side effect: pregnant women who took this drug did not experience morning sickness. It was an Eureka moment. An over-the-counter drug could prevent morning sickness. Unaware of what was happening in their uterus, these pregnant women went about their lives, awaiting the birth of their darling babies. Little did they anticipate the shock that awaited them. The babies were born with phocomelia—absent limbs or non-functional flipper-like limbs. Even then, it took time for people to associate this condition with the consumption of thalidomide in early pregnancy. By then, it was too late and hundreds of families suffered with the birth of a child with phocomelia. Fortunately, no one in India would have had this experience, as women back then did not take supplements easily during pregnancy. Call it culture or lack of information, it was difficult to convince pregnant women to take even the necessary supplements.

But imagine a life without limbs or non-functional limbs! We are born as bipeds; our minds are geared to doing fine activities with our fingers. How does one perform the simplest of tasks like walking and eating? How does one write or turn the pages of a book? And all the four limbs missing? Kent Bell has written about his experiences as an individual with no limbs in *Look Ma, No Hands, No Legs Either*—an inspirational, touching and practical book which inspired the title to this story.

In my very early days as an Iyengar Yoga teacher, I was an observer-cum-assistant in the medical classes at Ramamani Iyengar Memorial Yoga Institute (RIMYI), Pune, where people with all kinds of disorders/diseases came to seek freedom from their conditions. Most had not succeeded with conventional treatment and had come to RIMYI as a last resort with a lot of hope. The medical classes at RIMYI involved Guruji himself guiding the students. In some cases, he would personally help them; in some, he would ask the senior teachers; and sometimes he would assign some tasks to novices like me. 'Make this person do Trikonasana.' And we would follow Guruji's instruction. Then, Guruji would make subtler adjustments and the expression on the patient's face would change. I soon realised that it was not the asana but the finer adjustments that gave relief. We needed to learn to 'read' the patient's facial as well as skin expression. It was relatively easy to observe the face but it took me a long time to read the skin—its colour, texture and the direction of extension. The teachers or trainee teachers were assigned one or two patients whom they had to look after. Guruji would swiftly walk from one end of the hall to the other, adjusting somebody, advising somebody, moving from patient to patient. It surprised a novice like me that, with over sixty to seventy patients in the hall, he remembered what each one suffered from and what advice he had already given them and then proceeded from that. There was no time for questions, which anyway, I admit, I did not have the courage to ask.

So in my first few medical classes, I followed Guruji like a shadow, trying to make sense of what he was doing or saying. Along with me were a bunch of similar students. To be honest, none of us really knew why he did what he did. One, none of us had his depth, and two, he was too quick! Just following him across the hall made us tired after the two-hour class. If I had a smartphone then, I am sure it would have complimented me for completing my target of walking! Sometimes, we would be cheeky and ask the patient or the caregiver what problem the patient suffered from. The regulars ignored us. It was like a senior doctor's rounds in the hospital. The patients and family members were looking for words of wisdom from the consultant and not questions from an over-smart intern.

While I followed Guruji, I wondered whether he noticed me. But then I was raw and immature and had not realised that he could see things even if his gaze was not on that object or person. One day, suddenly, he turned and told me, 'Make him do Ardha Chandrasana.' Wow! Guruji had trust in me and had assigned a patient to me! What was wrong with this patient? What was his medical history? Why should I make him do Ardha Chandrasana? In what way would it help him? My mind asked these questions but they were never converted into speech. Guruji never encouraged superficial questions. He believed in action. If a person was suffering and had approached us for freedom from that pain, our job as a teacher or an assistant was to deliver that.

So I looked at the person and guided him to do Ardha Chandrasana with the support of a trestle. In this asana, the practitioner spreads the feet apart, turns one leg, say the right one, ninety degrees outward and places the right palm in line but approximately one foot away from the right foot. Then, the left leg is raised such that it becomes parallel to the floor. Basically, the practitioner balances on one leg with the support of the palm. And to improve balance, the person's back is rested on a support such as a wall or a trestle.

I instructed the patient and helped him correctly place the foot and the palm and lift the other leg up. I was thrilled when the patient did the asana. He came down after a while and I made him repeat it. Then, I waited for Guruji to return from his round of the class and give us further instructions. Guruji came back while the patient was still in the pose, nodded, asked me to make him do the asana on the other side and walked away. *Other side?* This patient had only one leg. The other was amputated from the thigh down! How could I make him do the asana on the other side? Had Guruji not noticed, my naïve mind questioned. But that did not seem possible. Guruji was so observant! I waited next to the patient. This was his first class, so he too did not have any clue what to do.

Guruji came back and asked, 'Did you make him do the asana on the other side?' I garnered courage to say, 'Sir, he has only one leg.' Now I seemed to have triggered Guruji's anger. He replied, 'So?' I was thoroughly confused. How could I make a man balance on one leg when the leg did not even exist? I was totally blank, lost. My joy of being observed and trusted by Guruji faded and turned into fear and a feeling of stupidity. I waited. Guruji gave me a very stern, angry look, but his eyes expressed compassion. He asked me to get a stool and placed the 'stump' of the amputated leg on the stool. He placed a couple of blankets under the stump so that the hip of the patient's affected leg was in line with the hip of the lifted leg. And thus the patient was balancing in Ardha Chandrasana on a leg which did not exist. Wow! How did I not think of this?

My thoughts were distracted by the expression on the patient's face. He showed signs of relief. Guruji said, 'He would have so much pain in the back and the hips since the leg has been amputated.' The patient nodded with a smile. Then Guruji left, saying, 'Now continue.' I was genuinely mesmerised. Why had I not thought of that? The man had severe pain in the hip and back and that was the reason he was in the therapy class. Guruji had not asked him anything, neither interviewed him nor noted his history. He could just look at the patient, feel his pain and give him the right action to provide relief. I must admit that, until then, I respected Guruji, but mainly because the world did too. This incident opened my eyes and my mind made me bow down to him.

I understood why the legs are called karmendriya—organs of action. The legs play such a big role in the health of the spine and the hips. A pain in the hips and the back may be reflected in the legs and a problem in the legs could be due to a nerve impingement in the spine. Guruji had not looked at visuals of the nerves that emerged from the various vertebrae nor had he looked at videos or scanned the internet. It was all from his own experience.

I came back to the medical class a few weeks later and saw that the man was smiling and happy. He then mentioned that he had pain in his missing limb. In this phenomenon called phantom limbs, pain exists in the limb that does not exist. I learned that when amputees experience pain in the non-existent limb or limbs, it is not their imagination, but a real pain. Imagine two such limbs. Ironically, you cannot even move them because of their absence, yet they not only cause mental agony but physical pain too.

Many decades later, in December 2014, I met Mark Zambon. We had decided to celebrate Geetaji's seventieth birthday with what appealed to her most—teaching yoga. An event named 'Yoganushasanam—the yogic discipline' was planned in the badminton halls of Balewadi Stadium. Devastatingly, Guruji B.K.S. Iyengar had left his mortal body on 20 August 2014. But we distracted ourselves from this loss by getting more involved in the preparation of the event in which more than twelve hundred students from over fifty countries were to participate.

I handled most of the correspondence with the students and I received a request that a student named

Mark Zambon needed a chair for his practices during Yoganushasanam. While we do use a chair as a prop in Iyengar Yoga—it helps us stay longer in certain asanas and we can therefore go deeper in the asana and experience the other states of yoga—we avoid using such props during such big conventions for logistical reasons. Furthermore, Yoganushasanam was to be held in the badminton hall, and the authorities had clearly forbidden us from using anything sharp on the floor. Thus, there was no question of a chair.

However, this request intrigued me as we were told that Mark needed a chair to get into Shirshasana. Using a chair for Sarvangasana was common and two chairs for Shirshasana was advised for people with neck pain. But a single chair for Shirshasana? Despite three-and-a-half decades of yoga practice, I had no clue as to why or how one could use a single chair for Shirshasana.

Anyway, consent was granted to Mark Zambon, a student from San Diego, US. He had been introduced to Iyengar Yoga in a rehabilitation centre. Just thirty years old, he had lost both his legs and an arm in America's war in Afghanistan. Mark had enlisted as a marine in the American troops that were sent into Afghanistan to capture Osama bin Laden and his group of terrorists. A strong, fearless young man answering the call of his nation, Mark was not bothered by the fact that war and injuries go hand in hand. Then, he became the victim of a bomb blast and he was forced to return to California for rehabilitation.

The word rehabilitation cannot communicate all that needs to be rehabilitated. As a war veteran, you do have access to the best gadgets and treatment, but the most basic tasks become impossible. Moreover, besides claiming three of his limbs, the explosion had burnt more than 70 per cent of his skin. Imagine the burning sensation when a hot ladle or iron pan touches our tender skin on the palm or the forearm. We rush to cool it with water. For more severe burns, doctors initially try to prevent an infection and then long-term contracture. Burnt skin leaves scars which restrict the movement of the joints. We take many things in life for granted, including our body parts. We don't know their functions and we realise their importance only when they stop working. So it is with the skin, our largest sense organ which protects the body, regulates temperature and makes joint movement easy.

The explosion changed everything for Mark, a young man who worked out, spent time outdoors and had a strong body. Even the smallest of tasks needed to be relearnt.

Imagine getting into bed. What is the big deal? Lift the duvet, sit on the bed, lift the legs up, move them under the duvet, adjust the pillow, cover yourself with the duvet and then read or go to sleep. I'm sure people don't give too much thought to the 'methodology' of getting into bed. Neither had Mark.

After the explosion, the hospital staff and paramedics helped him in this task. But when he returned home, it was unimaginably tough. He was given a high-quality motorised wheelchair with the help of which he could move to the side as well as back and forth. The chair took him to the bed. But how could he move from the chair to the bed? He had to throw himself on the bed and depending on where he landed, he had to move his head to the pillow and cover himself. With two arms, he could have at least pushed himself to the right location. With just one functional arm, the only option was to roll and roll and roll till he reached the destination. The simplest of tasks, like getting into bed, had become very complex. And achieving this goal was not sufficient for a good night's sleep.

With 70 per cent of his skin burnt, Mark's body could not regulate his temperature in keeping with the environment. He felt very, very warm and sweaty, heating up with the smallest activity. Life was surely going to be tough. Dreams shattered, outdoor activities restricted, his childhood desire to climb Mount Kilimanjaro would have to be given up. It was depressing. But a soldier never gives up, and with the support of the best prosthetics, he decided to see how far life would normalise.

In a rehabilitation session, two months after the explosion, Mark befriended a Vietnam War veteran who informed Mark that his wife and her friend taught Iyengar Yoga in the rehabilitation centre on Tuesday afternoons. It seemed that those veterans who practised yoga felt that it gave them the experience of life. Mark joined that Iyengar Yoga class with many war veterans, disabled and without limbs, practising yoga on their beds. He loved the first experience and, continuing these sessions, became a regular.

In his own words, 'All these poses that I did allowed the body to heal properly. On top of that, on the mental side, the practice of Iyengar Yoga produces a sensation of whole-body wellness. You feel a state of great health. Your senses are sharpened, your vision, your hearing, your sense of smell—just a feeling of great well-being. So it was the combination of all this. Iyengar Yoga was a pillar, the key to my rehabilitation. It has basically brought me to the point where I am now, almost four years later, where I have worked through this process of recovery and the grief; where I have accepted my injury and realised that I am very fortunate to be here, to be alive.'

After a few classes, true to his nature, Mark was not happy to just do the asanas on the bed; he wanted to do something more challenging, like Shirshasana, which he had seen in the yoga books. His teacher took up the challenge and helped him up into Shirshasana. Lo and behold, the phantom limb pain diminished!

Initially, non-medicos believed that a person complaining of phantom limb pain was imagining it due to trauma—I wonder what is more painful, the pain itself or people's disbelief? Although phantom pain was first described by sixteenth-century French physician Ambroise Paré and later confirmed by the famous philosopher René Descartes, the science behind it was known only in the late 1990s. It is caused by alterations in neural connections. The treatment varies from regular use of painkillers to the more invasive deep brain or spinal cord stimulation. So it was indeed a revelation for Mark when the pain just disappeared as he did his Shirshasana. He soon developed a liking for this asana and wanted to do it more and hold it for longer.

Coincidentally, he received his prosthetic limbs at about the same time that he started learning Shirshasana. Both were strange sensations—seeing the world upside down and trying to hold on to something that was not his, the prosthetic limbs. It was as if the will power that he was developing to stay in Shirshasana was helping him adapt to and accept the prosthetic limbs better. The training of his mind through Shirshasana was helping in the training of the 'legs', and he soon took well to both. His first goal after the disaster was to climb Mount Kilimanjaro. With the highest peak at 19,000 feet, it is a tough climb even for experienced climbers; it would not be cakewalk for a thirty-year-old healthy individual, let alone one on prosthetic limbs. But Mark did it. Then he did his Shirshasana at 19,000 feet—the Shirshasana which had assisted him in accepting and making the prosthetics a part of his own body.

There is a false belief among so-called intellectuals that asanas are for the body and the higher aspects of ashtanga yoga are for the mind. We hear a catchy phrase—mind over body. To me, these are superficial words and the people who say it are in a make-believe world. Both mind and body are so closely integrated that you cannot differentiate except in terminology. When you 'work' on the body, you also 'work' on the mind. If the body develops endurance, so does the mind. If the body develops a sharp, discriminative intelligence where you can feel and identify each and every part of your body, then you develop that same sharpness in your mind. While working on the body in an asana, one is subtly working on the mind. If you are working with a lot of precision as demanded by Guruji and Iyengar yoga, you develop those traits in the mind. When you align the body, you align the mind too.

The one challenge that Mark faced was going up into Shirshasana on his own. People with limbs like us place the feet on the floor to adjust the shoulders and the trunk. Mark needed to rest his prosthetic legs on a bed or chair and adjust his shoulders and trunk to take his prosthetics up.

Apart from Geetaji who led the December 2014 convention like the sun, Mark was another star. He would go unnoticed if he was in any asana, including Shirshasana, except when you glanced at his legs and realised they were prosthetics.

While Mark continues his journey in life, fulfilling his aspirations, giving hope and inspiration to his fellow war veterans to relearn to live, he has left an indelible mark on my life.

Who are we to complain when a man can stand up from a condition where he is almost broken and achieve feats that even 'normal' people cannot? We all have been given the tools of yoga by Guruji. These tools, or sadhana, were like a code language in Patanjali's second chapter of the yoga sutras—the Sadhana Pada. Guruji decoded the mysticism and made them practical for ordinary mortals. If people like Mark can relive life, then imagine the scope for all of us. Except that we need perseverance like Mark!

Light Is Heard

> *The highest form of sensitivity is the highest form of intellect.*
>
> –B.K.S. Iyengar

I was in Tel Aviv a decade back, and my friends invited me to a restaurant, supposedly one of the most sought-after restaurants in the country. I was not told where I was being taken, but I fully trusted my hosts. They knew I was a vegetarian and they respected my sensibilities and sensitivities. Israel has a lot of vegetarian food, salads and baked stuff, and I was ready to try the local food. As it was supposed to be a special place, it made sense for me to dress up too.

We drove down to the restaurant. There was a café outside and a small, nondescript entrance to the restaurant. At the reception, my friends conversed in Hebrew with the person there—it appeared they were confirming our reservation.

Then, we walked into an anteroom which had many small lockers. We were asked to remove and store away our watches and jewellery and for that matter anything that shone. This was strange, I thought. They reassured us that all would be safe and we put our watches, earrings, purses and mobile phones in the locker. I was a bit concerned when we walked through a poorly lit narrow passage—I do not like dark restaurants and bars. I like to see my food and read the expressions on the faces of those accompanying me.

A young man in a black shirt and black trousers came up, introduced himself and told us that he would be accompanying us to the dining area. From outside, I could hear a lot of chatter, the sound of cutlery and plates and the clink of glasses. It appeared to be a very lively place. People seemed to be enjoying the ambience as well as the food and the drink.

Inside the room, it was pitch dark, as though the lights had just gone out. I froze. Our eyes generally adapt to darkness in a few moments and we regain our bearings. But here, even that was not possible as there was not even a glimmer of light, not even a small light bulb or any light creeping in from a window. My guide took my hand, placed it on his shoulder and asked me to follow him.

The sounds of people chatting continued around us and I found that I could not move. These same sounds that had given me pleasure and anticipation of a nice ambience a few moments ago, were not pleasant anymore—they were suddenly scary.

Till then I had not realised the role light and vision play in preventing fear. According to the yoga sutras, one of the five afflictions that all humans suffer from is the fear of death. What was interesting for me was that the sound that was pleasant in the presence of light and vision had given rise to fear in their absence.

I now realised why Guruji had asked us to teach Shavasana with the eyes open, to the earthquake victims in Kutch—something that is never done in our regular yoga classes. It also made sense why Guruji laid so much emphasis on keeping the eyes open while teaching people with depression. Closing the eyes triggers thoughts, which in their cases are of the negative kind.

Those first few moments drove my thoughts to the connection between the senses. When the vision is restricted, the hearing becomes sharper. This is why the visually impaired have a better sixth sense—the sense of proprioception. Guruji told us that the senses distract the mind by taking it outwards, but in the practice of yoga, these same senses take a U-turn and we begin our journey inward.

Later, when my analytical frontal brain got activated, I received loads of explanations, connections and understanding of our own behaviours, but at that moment, the part of my brain associated with the basic instinct of fear got activated. I was moving in super-slow motion, concentrating on each step. The sounds were distracting, and I needed to put all my attention into my steps in the darkness.

My guide was also walking slowly, but I was slower. When my hand slipped off his shoulder, I refused to move. 'Please wait,' I said. I was on firm ground, walking through a passage with people beside me; there was no logical reason for this fear. But emotions have no logic. My guide came up and made just one statement, 'Madam, don't get scared. Many of us spend our entire life in this manner.'

It then dawned on me that my guide was blind. I had barely walked for a few minutes in total darkness in the passage of a restaurant, that too with an escort. Imagine walking for decades through unknown areas without anybody to guide you, and yet living, not merely surviving.

I have visited thousands of restaurants but none has impacted me like this restaurant called BlackOut, which touched a different chord inside me. It is a part of an organisation called Na Lagaat, meaning, please do touch.

We did not have any food in BlackOut. But I had a lot of food for thought. Outside the restaurant was a café where deaf people served food and all we had to do was either speak slowly or point at what we wanted. We surely use our eyes much more than our ears. Is this the reason that more people need aids for their eyes early on in life than aids for the ears? Are we silencing our other senses because we are not using them sufficiently and not letting them evolve, especially the forgotten sixth sense?

We are all familiar with the five senses of sight, sound, touch, smell and taste, but some of us are not very familiar with the sixth sense of proprioception. Proprioception is our inbuilt capability to know the position and the movement of our body with reference to the external environment. Take this simple test of proprioception. Close your eyes and move your index finger towards your nose. Even without a mirror, we can easily move the index finger to the tip of the nose. But in case of some neurological limitations, we may not be able to do it, just like with some other neurological limitations, we are not able to see.

However, even if we pass this basic test, our proprioception is poor. I doubt whether any of us can walk with the same speed with our eyes closed in our own homes as we do with our eyes open. Should we then call the visually impaired as people with a high sense of proprioception or a high PQ (proprioception quotient)?

The question is whether proprioception can be cultivated. After all, we can exercise our muscles and various faculties, and we tend to lose certain abilities if we don't use them often. Take the example of memorising phone numbers. A generation earlier, people could memorise many phone numbers with ease; today, with mobile phones, we cannot recollect even five. Likewise, with a more frequent use of GPS, we may lose our sense of navigation.

A decade ago, a young German yoga practitioner, Birgit Andrews, did show that it was possible to develop this sense of proprioception. Back then I did not even know that such a term existed.

Stand erect, with your feet and toes together, and close your eyes. Within a few moments, you will feel that you are swaying. While balance is influenced by the ears, the vestibular organs, you will find that the eyes play a role too. Imagine walking with your eyes closed in a plain field, where there is no fear of banging into something or tripping over—a sense of imbalance will still exist. Imagine trying to learn a new activity like yogasana with the eyes closed. My imagination totally failed.

If I want to learn or teach any yogasana, the eyes play the primary role. I either open a copy of *Light on Yoga* or watch a demonstration given by a teacher. When we teach beginners, we ensure that their eyes are wide open as we perform the asana before them. In fact, the power of the eyes over the ears becomes evident in cases where words and visuals don't match. For example, if a teacher asks the students to extend their arms but the teacher's arms are themselves bent, the students imitate the teacher's bent arms. Or suppose a teacher is demonstrating Trikonasana, facing the students. If she bends to the right and verbally asks the students to bend to their right, surprisingly, many would bend to the left, mirroring the teacher. Learning and teaching yoga both seemed nearly impossible in the absence of vision. Of course, one could instruct orally and make do with whatever the student did, thinking 'at least, they are doing something'. This is often out of a sense of sympathy for their limitation or contentment with their effort. But Birgit Andrews was different. She was not content with just the effort. Instead, she developed and mastered proprioception to a level beyond imagination.

Birgit was lean and tall and blonde. She generally wore red t-shirts and shorts for yoga class. Most of the time, her sense of colour was very good, and her clothes were perfectly matched. However, she could not see colour; in fact, she was blind. It seemed as though nature had endowed her with a special sense of touch whereby she could associate the texture of the clothes with the colour.

The fact was that she, like most of us, was not born with a heightened sense of touch. She was born with normal vision and a love for colours. An accident at the age of twenty-two took away her vision but not her love or sensitivity. She had to learn how to see with her inner eyes, and she did.

The basic human instinct is to survive. Imagine being in such a situation. We would take each step cautiously, slowing down, using our hands to ensure that we don't bump into anything or stumble. Moving ahead requires a beautiful blend of courage and caution—a lesson on how to live life. We need courage to go beyond mediocrity, not recklessness. We need to take a bold step to move ahead but with a lot of caution—a balance between the two leads to progress.

Birgit was an active person like most young people and loved movement, whether in the form of classical dance or skiing. The accident brought an end to these activities. Using the body to even walk—a simple movement we take for granted—was challenging. It was a big effort to retain balance and not fall down. Her first reaction was 'Why me?', a question which all who face trauma ask. But it has no answers. The only answer is to accept the situation and move on. If we don't, life becomes a burden.

She started life afresh trying to use the visual memory of her past life. For example, when she wanted a dress of a specific colour—twilight orange or the colour of fresh leaves—she felt the texture and started identifying her clothes, with help from her family and friends. Day-to-day activities progressed, but the joy of movement had to be given up. Survival was possible but living was difficult.

Living requires us to be in sync with our environment—with other humans, other inhabitants of the world and nature itself. The sense of proprioception tells us where we are with reference to the environment and it is only natural that we respect it. The beginning of the loss of balance is the start of disharmony with nature itself.

After eight years, a friend offered to take Birgit to an Iyengar Yoga class. She accepted the offer as yoga is to be done within the restricted space of a mat, which meant she could move without banging into something or falling. The practice of yoga did something far beyond what she had expected. It possibly developed an intense sense of proprioception. To understand how that happened, let us visualise a typical Iyengar Yoga class for beginners.

A class has anywhere between ten and fifty students. They are organised on the mats in such a way that the teacher who is in the front can see all of them. The teacher then calls the students closer and demonstrates an asana with basic instructions. Then, the students return to their mats, while the teacher goes to the front of the class and repeats the asana, this time with step-wise instructions, as the students follow. Here, the students use two senses: sight and sound. The students become a reflection of the teacher and eventually progress to doing a variety of asanas involving movements ranging from standing and sitting to forward extensions, backward arching, inversions and twisting.

Imagine Birgit in a similar class. It is not a very big class and she is allocated a position but she cannot use her sight. She is dependent only on the audio without the visual.

The class starts. 'Stand in Tadasana with your feet and toes together. Look down and make sure your feet are touching each other.' Most students look down and find that their toes are not touching properly, although they'd thought they were. Closing the eyes for Tadasana also brings unsteadiness and makes balance difficult. The body seems to sway from side to side. Imagine this state in one of the first asanas—what would happen with the others as one progressed. This was possibly Birgit's experience.

One could be sympathetic and let Birgit stand in whatever way she could and be happy that she was at least doing something. But life is not made of linear equations—doing 20 per cent of an asana does not yield a 20 per cent effect, just like taking 20 per cent of the prescribed dose of a medicine does not effect a 20 per cent cure. In fact, there would be no effect unless a minimal dose is consumed. With the practice of asanas, too, a posture will help only when it is done accurately and precisely.

Academic scholars who interpret the ancient Indian texts on the yoga sutras often mistake the factor of comfort. The first sutra on asanas, 'sthira sukham asanam', literally translated means stability, joy or pleasure or comfort, posture or yogic posture. It can be interpreted as being in any comfortable and stable position. Or, it can be being comfortable and stable in any position or posture. There is a vast difference between these two statements. The former is a compromised state where we choose a comfortable position, while the latter is a state where, by making changes in our own self, we become comfortable and stable in any position. The former restricts us to our 'comfort zone', the latter gives us the ability to extend our boundaries and attain the same composure even beyond the comfort zone.

Birgit could have just spread her feet a bit and attained her balance in Tadasana. Did it really matter if the feet and toes were not placed together? What would a distance of 1 cm make to her body, brain and senses? In practice, that 1 cm does make a world of difference within the frame of the body—while the body sways when the feet are together and the eyes closed, extending the back of the calves and the frontal thigh muscles gives as much stability as when the eyes are open. How does it happen? Well, proprioceptive receptors are located in the muscles and the tendons, and extending the muscles sends different signals to the brain to give us a state of balance. Since each asana extends different muscles, one can imagine the number of receptors that can be activated if one attempts to get stability in a variety of asanas without compromising or getting into the state of 'at least doing something'.

Thus started Birgit's journey with Tadasana.

Let us go to the next asana—Utthita Trikonasana. In this posture, we spread the legs 3 to 4 feet apart, turn the left foot inwards, the right leg outwards and extend the right arm towards the floor or the right ankle if we are not flexible. How would Birgit measure the distance between her feet or know how far her palm was from the ankle or the floor?

The next asana was Virabhadrasana II, where we turn the right leg outwards and bend it to make a ninety-degree angle. The teacher instructs, 'Bend your leg at the knee and make a right angle between the thigh and the calf. Your thigh should be parallel to the floor.' How would Birgit know whether she had achieved this? How much should the leg be bent? 'The knee has a tendency to move inwards—keep it in the centre!' Could she tell if hers had turned inwards? At these classes, the teachers would move her thigh down so that it was parallel to the floor. The touch of the teachers started giving her some idea on how to do the asanas. It was a challenge that she took up.

With time, more and more asanas were introduced. The movements of her body in the limited space of the mat was heartening and she continued with her classes. As instructions came from the teacher, questions popped up in her head. For Shirshasana, when the teacher said, 'Interlock the fingers and place the forearms and palms on the mat with the elbows as wide apart as the shoulders,' she wondered: 'How close are my elbows? Are they in line with the shoulders?' Fortunately, the teachers would physically adjust her elbows so that they were in line with her shoulders. This happened with all the postures. For the other students, the instructions from the teachers triggered their memories of bending the leg to make a right angle, of keeping a specific distance between the feet, and they could also see their own body parts. Birgit remembered the words, but the 'feeling' that came when the teacher adjusted the distance between her elbows in Shirshasana or between her feet in the standing asanas was very difficult to recollect. After all, objective learning is much easier than subjective learning. But the teachers were patient and so was Birgit and her journey in yoga continued.

Slowly, she started becoming independent in class and did not require much physical help from the teachers. By staying within the boundary of her mat, she also overcame her fear of banging into somebody or tripping. The mat became her space after a friend or a fellow practitioner walked her to it. She did not need any more physical help from the fellow practitioners. It was a nice feeling to be independent. But another problem came up—acquiring the sense of direction. Once on the mat, she did not know which direction she was facing. While the entire class was facing the teacher, she could land up with her back to the teacher or stand angularly. But what are neighbours for? They would quickly grip her hand and turn her around. She was saved from what she felt were embarrassing moments. Her confidence was building up. She was in the confines of her mat. She was facing the right direction, thanks to her neighbours.

But the right orientation was still missing. Here, the mat became her greatest asset. It set the boundaries and it gave the orientation and the alignment that Iyengar Yoga has gained recognition for. She used it as her 'eyes'. If the hall was rectangular, then she could place the short edge of the mat such that it touched the wall, automatically making it straight. If the wall was on the left, she knew that if she touched the outer edge of her left foot to the wall, she would be facing the front. But how would she know whether she was slightly angular? Again, the mat came to her rescue. Standing on the front edge of the mat, she knew whether her feet were straight or at an angle. In Urdhva Dhanurasana, how would she know whether the palms were in line? Here too, the mat became her white cane. She realised that if she folded the mat twice and touched the edge of her palms and feet to the mat—she had to be straight. She had started developing her own means to overcome her limitations of vision.

Little did she know that she was not just coping with her condition but developing a whole new dimension of inner attention and inner vision. She realised that while people saw their bodies from the outside, she had to feel her arms, legs and trunk from the inside and align them. This was a great struggle. While the others aligned with their vision, she had to align them with the internal touch and despite all her efforts, it was very difficult. She tried hard to get that internal alignment which she felt all the other students in the class must be achieving just by following the teacher's instructions and demonstration. Of course, this was not true.

Take the example of Trikonasana. As beginners, the eyes of the students catch that the teacher has placed the right palm on the floor. They imitate that, but at the cost of the rest of the body—the trunk could be leaning forward, the right buttock pushed backward and even the legs might be bent at the knees. It is a posture, but there is no stability in the body, mind and senses—there is no 'sthira sukham asanam'. This is just doing a posture. But Guruji and Iyengar Yoga, which later became associated with precision and alignment, did not accept such casual practice of postures. We have to feel both sides of the body. If we extend the arms to the side, the feeling has to be the same in both the arms, even in the upper and the lower arm. It is only with time that we start using the subjective feeling to get towards precise alignment. But Birgit had started with the subjective feeling and, unbeknownst to her, she was progressing much better than she thought till she was in front of Guruji's eyes.

Birgit had been attending classes and large conventions, and in 1993, she attended the one at the Crystal Palace, London, which was taught by Guruji himself. In the class of over a thousand people, Guruji noticed this lady who was precisely following and implementing his teachings in her asanas consistently. He called her on the stage and made her perform the asana along with some senior teachers. It was soon noticed how this young German exhibited precision, which Germans are famous for, in her asanas.

She was appreciated and applauded, not because she was doing 'something' despite being blind, but because she was doing it better than those with vision. It was indeed a big boost to her confidence.

How did Birgit do it? She did it with inner vision and inner attention. Psychologists today recognise the different parts of the brain that are activated by our attention—the pre-frontal cortex for outward attention on an object and the posterior cingulate cortex in the middle region of the brain for attention directed inwards. Birgit learnt subjectively. Both subjective and objective learning are important. Objectivity brings ease of expression and assessment; it is more structured but lacks sensitivity. Subjectivity generates finesse and develops clarity, balance and a discriminative intelligence. But subjective learning is always more difficult than objective learning.

It is only in the second decade of the twenty-first century that functional neuroimaging is making it possible to understand the areas of the brain involved in developing different attributes and how senses beyond the basic five play a role in our evolution. It makes me wonder how Guruji knew all this. Why did he insist on precision in yoga practice? How did he have the confidence that regular practice would transform individuals? It was simply through his own experience and his ability to develop his sixth sense so strongly that he could teach people to sense.

Birgit continues with her practice. Her friends asked her to teach, and she soon started with a few students. Now, fifteen years later, she teaches a class of forty with the assistance of her brother as and when required. She needs to know before class about new or outside students so that she 'knows' whom she is teaching.

Guruji said, 'Extension brings space, space brings freedom, freedom brings precision. Precision is truth. It is through the alignment of the body that I discovered the alignment of my mind, self and intelligence.'

When the Earth Quakes

Try to find comfort even in discomfort.

–B.K.S. Iyengar

Sunday, 26 January 2001. The fiftieth Republic Day of India. A day on which our forces display their military prowess on the Rajpath in Delhi. Many urban Indians take this day as an opportunity to relax or go off on a short holiday to refresh themselves. Nothing was different on this golden jubilee of the Indian Republic.

I admit that I belong to the category of the urban Indian who decided to take the day off. I took a bus on Friday night to the lush green tea estates in a place called Suryanelli in Kerala to spend the weekend in my friend

Shalaka's home. My intention was to soak myself in nature and maybe just relax with a book and a cup of tea. It was a big plan to do nothing. Mobile phones had not yet invaded my life, so it was easy to stay away from work.

That morning, to implement my grand plan of doing nothing, I picked up my cup of tea from the kitchen and was walking to the garden when I glanced at the 'breaking news' on television. An earthquake of magnitude 8.2 on the Richter scale had struck the western parts of India with its epicentre in Bhuj in the state of Gujarat. Although I lived in Mumbai and worked in Bangalore, Gujarat is where my parents came from and I had lots of family living there. My heart skipped a beat. I hoped none of them was affected; that there had not been any losses or injuries. I listened carefully to the newsreader list the areas of Gujarat that were affected and I heaved a sigh of relief that not much damage was reported where my relatives lived. I called home and this information was confirmed. My eyes went back to the television, where visuals of the areas damaged kept playing. I was sympathetic towards those affected by the calamity, but soon I went back to my original plan, before this interruption, of sitting in the garden and reading my book.

In hindsight, I realise how self-centred I was. We are concerned for ourselves, our close family, our friends, our acquaintances, and that is it. On the other hand, what would have been the point of being 'bothered' if there was nothing I could do? I was not going to take away the pain of the unknown thousands by feeling sad and unhappy. And what could I do, siting so far away?

We are not really too concerned about the rest of the human race, let alone other species on the planet. I have used the word 'we' intentionally, as I believe that this is the behaviour of most of us—if not, the world would be a different space! This realisation came to me many years later when I watched the news of the terrorist attack on the American Embassy in Kenya. The American representative kept talking about the safety of the Americans—there was nothing about the Kenyan staff. But whichever part of the world we live in, this is human nature, including my own.

The earthquake did shake me up for a few moments, but then the news became information which was disconnected from my emotions and I went back to my plans of a holiday in the lush hills of Kerala. The rest of the day went off uneventfully for me as well as for millions of Indians, except for those in the state of Gujarat.

Over the next few days, we kept reading about the extent of damage that this earthquake had left behind—over a lakh lives were lost. The greatest damage had occurred in the province of Kutch, to a community which had learnt to live in their desert terrain. There was no count on the number injured, especially grave head injuries and broken bodies. In a few seconds, generations were wiped out; entire villages were destroyed. But the stories of survival and pain, which initially appeared on the front pages of newspapers, were gradually relegated to the inner pages, then to a few columns and finally to weekly reports.

In any case, it was mere information. Honestly, it is very difficult to 'feel' the gravity of such a situation unless you have had a similar personal experience. I did not have such memories, and I must admit that though I felt sympathetic when I read the news, my sympathies were superficial—honest but not honestly from the heart. Life moved on with this date etched in history and loosely in my memory like any other news article whose impact would fade with time.

But although human nature tends to be self-centred, our conscience does want us to help those who are suffering. In the case of natural disasters, we try to help in whatever way we can. Usually, all we can do is give some money. Our institute, Ramamani Iyengar Memorial Yoga Institute (RIMYI), started receiving appeals for donations in cash and kind as many national and international agencies started relief operations and people from all walks of life collected donations.

Guruji B.K.S. Iyengar taught us by example, donating a sum of ten lakh rupees, along with tonnes of food items. He also donated a lot of his personal belongings, including newly stitched silk kurtas and finely embroidered new shawls he had received as tokens of honour from organisations and individuals. Guruji lived by his own principle: 'Giving does not impoverish and withholding does not enrich.' What else could one expect from a yogi who strives to see the truth? He was not attached to anything. The volunteers were touched. Many students were in tears as Guruji so easily emptied his cupboards of material possessions as well as honours bestowed on him. Some offered to take those mementoes and pay for them in cash. Motivated, his students in Pune and Mumbai too started their own collection drives.

The trucks left for Gujarat. And our lives started returning to normal while the people of Gujarat and the relief agencies worked to rebuild the lives of those afflicted. Only time would tell whether these places would revive or become buried cities for archaeologists to study. Time would tell whether the people would restart their lives in other lands and how many of them would live fully, rather than merely surviving. Time would also heal the wounds but leave some scars. My involvement with the earthquake, whose shock waves were felt as far as China in the east and Chennai in the south, ended with the trucks leaving Pune for Gujarat—at least that is what I presumed.

Two weeks later, I received a phone call. 'Hello, we got your number from Mr Rao and we seek your assistance for the victims of the earthquake in Gujarat.'

I promptly replied, without giving the caller any time to say another word, 'We have already sent relief material and donations to Gujarat.' I wondered how people could be so greedy even during disasters. Rumours about fraudulent collection drives had been circulating, and I felt I was smart not to fall prey to such scamsters.

It turned out to be a wrong presumption. The caller said that they did not want any money or material. I asked, 'Then how can I help you?'

The caller replied, 'The people in our camp have been provided with everything—clothes, food, blankets—but they are very depressed. We were wondering whether you could teach them yoga to help them out of their emotional distress.'

I promptly said, 'Yes, of course. We can help in whatever way possible.' And in the next few minutes, a tentative plan was made with Mr Asif Khan of the Aga Khan Foundation. We would be sending yoga teachers to the relief camp in the village of Nagalpur, which had over four hundred residents, and to other camps in Bhuj, Anjar and Bhachau.

My mind went into a tizzy, micro-planning the project. We would send three or four teachers every week for four to five weeks, starting on 10 March. I presumed that all my fellow teachers would be happy to serve and share our Guruji's teachings with these unfortunate ones. We would take the evening train from Mumbai and reach Gandhinagar the next afternoon. Mr Khan would arrange for transport from the station to the camp, as well as our accommodation and food. As for props, we would send spare blankets from the silver jubilee celebrations of our institute the year before. Even as I made the plans, my mind questioned, 'Can we teach yoga in such conditions?' I immediately called up Guruji and asked him. He said, 'Yes.' And a commitment was made to the Aga Khan Foundation.

Back in 2001, yoga was not as well known to the common man in urban India and abroad, let alone in the villages. In fact, on his eightieth birthday in 1998, Guruji had expressed his desire to take yoga to the villages in India.

At our next yoga class, I announced that we needed volunteers to teach in Gujarat. I was excited about this unique project. Many hands went up—some were teachers, some were assistant teachers and some just wanted to help out. I promptly noted their names and availability.

The more pragmatic people in our group raised questions about our accommodation in the relief camp and our experience in teaching disaster survivors. They doubted that the people in the camp would want to do yoga when they were likely to be more concerned about arranging for day-to-day requirements like food and shelter. I did not have any answers ready for my colleagues. I was acting on the faith that Guruji and Mr Khan had. We would ask Guruji about our plan of action, and, though I had had only one conversation with him, I thought that Mr Khan would take care of the rest of the arrangements.

So, undeterred by the questions, I said that we had plenty, and it was time to give back. Many thought the exercise was futile though, and some said they were unable to take leave from work or responsibilities at home. Finally, a list of twenty volunteers was made and divided into five batches.

But our enthusiasm was soon dampened by the reality and practical concerns about our experience in dealing with natural disasters or trauma. My only memory of a disaster was running down the steps of our building as a child during the Koynanagar earthquake. People stood on the dark street with some of their possessions and, a few minutes later, went back into their houses. It was like a midnight walk!

I had absolutely no clue about the situation at the camp. When we get so jittery on losing a book, some money or a gift from a loved one, how would it feel to have lost everything? We feel so upset when a piece of porcelain breaks; what about when everything we own is broken and turned into rubble? If losing something is difficult to handle, then how does one handle losing everything? I could not fathom the state of mind on experiencing such loss. I was fortunate to have had a comfortable life in modern India, and my only brush with trauma and bereavement was when I lost my mother to an ailment and medical negligence five years ago. It had taken me a long while to move on in life. What could I do or say to a group of people who had lost many if not all of their near and dear ones—what could I say to a lone surviving child of a family or a mother who had lost all her children in literally a few seconds? I felt as though I were a mere pawn in the game of 'imagine if', without any answers or options.

I soon discerned the reality of what I had walked into and realised that I needed help. My friend Anita and I went to meet an eminent psychiatrist, Dr Harish Shetty, who was an expert in disaster psychology and had worked with several survivors. He gave prudent advice on post-traumatic stress disorder, a term I had never heard about till then. For victims or witnesses to traumatic experiences, the minutest of triggers could bring back memories of the moment of trauma and cause extreme anxiety. This was called post-traumatic stress disorder. He explained that, for victims of earthquakes, noise is the biggest trigger. Any loud sound could trigger a fear of another quake. He also advised us to be very cautious during any conversation with the victims, since their emotions were still raw.

With this professional advice in our kitty, our group of volunteers went to Guruji for his practical advice and blessings. We were ready with our writing pads and pens, expecting Guruji to give us a list of asanas with modifications appropriate for such a condition. What followed was unexpected. The first thing that he told us was not to wear our regular yoga clothes—t-shirts and tights or shorts. Had we heard him correctly? What did

Guruji expect us to wear? 'You women should wear saris,' he said. We were surprised. Wear saris to teach yoga when none of us wore them regularly? Guruji said, 'Remember, all this while, you have been teaching yoga to people who have come to you. Now, you are going to a village under such circumstances and the people may not even be interested in yoga. They have to accept you first before you can reach out to them with this art.'

'But they have invited us to teach,' we said.

Guruji explained that the organisers were not the survivors of the earthquake. Our acceptance by the local people would depend upon how we presented ourselves. Only when we stayed with them, shared their food and dressed like them would they be willing to learn the art of yoga from us. This advice was well received by all of us; we negotiated with Guruji and finally decided that we would go neither in jeans nor in saris but in salwar kurtas.

Then, Guruji gave us more advice. We were to never ask them to close their eyes, not even in Shavasana. The darkness behind their closed eyes would remind them of the dark night when their world had turned, literally, upside down. This was to prevent 'memory recall'. And to overcome the anxiety that the memories triggered, they had to imagine two eyes on their temple and open those. We tried it ourselves and it did work. Then, he guided us on the asanas focussing on the opening of the chest—the emotional centre.

When I showed him the list of the volunteers who would go as a group of four for five weeks, he immediately told us that there should be an overlap between the batches so that the students were not faced with a new group of teachers every week. We were now all geared to go on our mission.

I sought Guruji's blessings, saying I would come back with the detailed report after five weeks. He said in a light tone, 'Whether there would be five weeks will depend upon how you fare in the first week!' It was a light statement with a heavy overtone.

In the first batch, I was to be the only person who taught classes regularly. My colleagues included a social worker, an assistant teacher and Anita, who taught medical classes. Indirectly, the onus was on Anita and me. I was charged up about this mission to give back to society. Little did I know that even if we want to give, there has to be somebody to receive.

The tickets had been booked and the spare blankets had been sent off so that they would reach before us. Mr Asif Khan was to accompany us from Mumbai Central station. Asif appeared to be in his early thirties. He was on crutches, with a leg in a cast. We were overwhelmed that he had come all the way from Bhuj to pick us up in such a condition.

As we made ourselves comfortable for the eighteen-hour overnight journey, we learnt from Asif the condition of the camps, six weeks after the disaster. We found out that he had not been injured in the quake but rather in Pune. He was as new to the terrain of Kutch as we were!

A vehicle had been arranged to take us to the Nagalpur camp from Gandhidham station and we reached the camp in the late afternoon. We saw that many huge tents had been pitched to accommodate over four hundred families, with two or three large families staying in each tent. There were barely any people around.

We were taken to meet a senior person, somebody akin to a village head, in the jamaat khana, which was a large tent with no furniture except a long low table. I thought that this was where we were to teach yoga. I was already planning to use the table for Setu Bandha Sarvangasana, a pose that would open up the chest well and make the camp people feel better.

The chief did not seem excited to receive us generous souls though! He asked us about our plans. We said we were at their service and could conduct morning and evening classes, in several batches even, in case of a big turnout. He did not respond. When I tried to confirm whether that tent could serve as the yoga hall, he answered with a flat 'no', it was the jamaat khana. My offer to reschedule the yoga classes in case they had other activities met with the same response. We were told that we could hold our classes outside. But outside, the ground was uneven, strewn with pebbles and stones, and the weather was inclement. The blankets would get dusty too. Blankets—what blankets? We learnt that the parcel with the blankets had not reached.

Again, I pleaded that the big tent was perfect; we could even use the table to do certain asanas. The chief looked at me as if I was crazy. 'You cannot do anything here.' I failed to grasp the problem.

Asif intervened, took me aside and explained that the jamaat khana was the place of worship for the people of the camp, who were all Ismailis. But yoga has nothing to do with religion—we had people of all religions in our classes in Pune and Mumbai. Why was he so apprehensive? I soon realised that, in times of disaster, we fall back on religion even if we are not religious or don't follow rituals. The relief camps had been organised by different socio-religious organisations for specific communities, and this camp was for the Ismailis. Some may call it discriminatory, but I felt that, in such times, when it was not possible to help all, it made practical sense to help one's community, who share similar beliefs and food habits.

So we were in a camp for the Muslim community, where the chief was not against yoga but definitely not excited about it either, possibly because it is often perceived as part of Hindu culture. However, perhaps our enthusiasm finally convinced him, and he permitted us to teach in the jamaat khana, provided we did nothing 'objectionable'—I deciphered it to mean no prayers, invocations and chanting auṁ. What a relief! We had come all the way and it was a small thing to give up!

Guruji had overcome similar challenges when Iyengar Yoga was introduced by the Inner London Education Authority. Since they did not want him to speak in Sanskrit and discuss philosophy, Guruji coined English names for the asanas and skipped the philosophy. But eventually, people who started practising the postures went back to the source. Now Western students not only learn the philosophy but also recite the yoga sutras.

A message about our yoga class was sent to the residents of the camp. Then, we went to our tent—our home for the next ten days. It was very spacious, furnished with five mattresses for the four of us and Asif. We were shown the makeshift toilets and informed that there was a tin shed for bathing. If we wanted something more 'concrete', we could use the bathroom in a house close by, but it was a good ten- or fifteen-minute walk. Once again, Asif enquired whether we really wanted to stay in the camp, and offered to arrange for a guest house a little farther away. Remembering Guruji's advice, we settled down in our tents, preparing for the evening class.

Very few students turned up at the jamaat khana. We believed it was because we had not had enough time to inform the residents. We walked to where people were carrying on with their day-to-day activities. Many were on kitchen duty, chopping tonnes of onions and cooking in humongous vessels out in the open. The women greeted us warmly and seemed to us to be offering tea, which we politely declined. It was soon dinner time. We had not been expecting much, but the yellow khichdi was surprisingly tasty.

The next morning, there were just about eight students—all teenagers. And there we were, four teachers for eight students! Guruji's words started ringing in my head. 'Whether there would be five weeks will depend upon how you fare in the first week.' What could we do if they did not come? We could not possibly drag them into the class.

As we walked around the camp, we spoke to a few women and invited them for the yoga class in the evening. Some looked blankly at us; some said that they did not need yoga since they were already working very hard in the camp. We were surprised that, despite their disinterest in what we wanted to do, they kept offering us tea at all times of the day. Or were we getting them wrong? Were they saying something else? We stopped a kid and asked her to slowly repeat what a woman had just said. It was their form of greeting: ya ali madad—may God bless you! We wanted to be accepted, so we tried to get the right diction and repeat it to the next person who walked by. But the next person was smarter and beat us to it by saying good morning before we could say ya ali madad!

What could we do to change the perception they had about yoga? We arranged for a talk in the jamaat khana in the evening. As Anita and I spoke about yoga and its benefits, they listened with unresponsive faces. I was almost pleading, extolling the benefits of yoga, when something struck a chord with them—that yoga would give them better sleep. The next morning, we had a few more students. We were progressing, but the pace was still too slow to create an impact.

Then, on our walk through the camp, I was approached by a woman who asked if I could help her father-in-law sleep. The seventy-seven-year-old man had lost his house where seven generations of his family had lived; he had lost his family business and heirloom books too. He had not slept for six weeks. Restless, he kept calling out to people at night, which meant that none of the four families in that tent could sleep. A student is an incarnation of God, Guruji had said. We visited the tent to teach the old man some asanas. The tent was overcrowded with miscellaneous items scattered all over. The only makeshift bed was made on a charpai, on which the man was lying down.

He was looking disinterestedly at the roof of the tent. He was very frail and had tremors due to Parkinson's. On top of that, we were told he did not eat much, and had become so weak that he could not even sit up. We had indeed taken up a challenge. I wore a mask of confidence, thinking fervently of ways to help him in such a condition and in a tent. We helped him to sit up on his 'bed' by putting a pillow lengthwise for his upper back, thereby raising the chest. The chest is the emotional centre—we had heard Guruji talk about this often—and a sunken chest means a sunken heart, physiologically and emotionally. We pressed his thighs down so he could breathe better while we waited with bated breath. Gradually, his tremors reduced and his face relaxed. My heart started beating faster. The old man opened his eyes and asked for his glasses to look at our faces. There were tears in the eyes of the daughter-in-law. This was the first time in six weeks that her father had smiled. We heaved a sigh of relief and my heart thanked Guruji. What an effect that simple adjustment had made!

The students from the morning class came back in the evening, so at least we were successful in maintaining our numbers!

The next morning was a pleasant surprise. Many more students had come. Was this a miracle? Had they all come for the yoga class? How did this transformation occur? How did we manage to convince them? They were all cooperative. Children were made to do inversions, especially Adho Mukha Vrikshasana, where they propped themselves up on their palms. One teacher stood behind, while another helped them up. They made endless queues, coming back again and again, giggling and laughing. Our arms were tired, but it was such a joy!

The lady whose father-in-law we had helped reported that for the first time since the earthquake, he had slept the entire night. The news had spread in the camp. She requested us to go back to help him, which we happily did. He was our saviour—how could we not? We were happy to see that he looked better just after sleeping one entire night.

I had spent years practising and teaching asanas, but this was the first time I had seen the power of a simple adjustment innovated by Guruji. We wondered how he had thought of something neither psychologists, nor physiotherapists, nor medical practitioners had.

Our social life in the camp got very busy, as requests to visit people with varying problems kept increasing. We started visiting several tents, in addition to conducting classes from 6.30 a.m. to 9.30 a.m., with over eighty students per class and two classes for children in the evening. The kids just loved the sessions. The schools had not reopened, so they kept following us around, even to our tent. We would keep the entrance to our tent closed to keep the heat, wind and sand out, and the kids' feet would bring sand and dirt onto our beds, but we did not have the heart to tell them anything. It was a joy to see them smiling and laughing.

Till then, we had communicated with them in Gujarati and Hindi. They now wanted to learn English. So we started English 'classes' on our beds. They repeated whatever we said. They had some exposure in school but could not communicate in English or practise it. So they took this opportunity to learn.

While we taught them yoga and English, we got many life lessons from these so-called victims or survivors, in turn. We hear pep talks on positive thinking, and here they were, people of all ages, living positively in the midst of extreme adversities. If I had to use the common analogy, they belonged to the category of optimists who think of the empty space in a half-full glass as an opportunity to fill fresh water.

One teenager told us that the earthquake had given them a lot. Was he being sarcastic? What had they got? He said, 'We were living in a small village where most of our people were farmers. We did go to a school but we had no access to modern amenities. After the earthquake, the Aga Khan Foundation has organised computer classes and yoga classes for us. We have had so many people from different fields come to talk to us. We would never have got the opportunity to learn all this, and that too from such experts.' The foundation had realised that it would be a while before houses and lives could be rebuilt, and the long wait could easily lead to depression. So they had organised lectures, doctor visits, computer classes and yoga classes to keep the minds of the youth occupied. They had indeed succeeded.

The residents of this area, Kutch, are called Kutchis. Having learnt over generations how to make friends with inhabitable, drought-ridden environs, they have a great business sense—many Kutchis who migrated to other parts of India, especially in Gujarat and Mumbai, can be found successfully running well-stocked grocery shops. Their indomitable spirit was visible here in the camp too. How long could they live at the mercy of people's goodwill and generosity? They needed support to rebuild their houses, but they also needed to get back to earning their livelihood. On a walk through the camp, we saw a woman sitting on a chair with a face pack and another getting her eyebrows shaped. A small beauty parlour had been started by some young women. If the clients did not have money, they bartered their services and skills. At the entrance to the camp, a small teashop had come up. It sold newspapers, soft drinks and a few items of daily use for the hundreds of visitors like us.

Over a cup of tea, the villagers one day chatted with us. 'What has happened is very sad. Something we must have done knowingly or unknowingly has brought upon us this wrath of nature. Maybe we were greedy, and this was our lesson. We have to bear it without moaning. People come and talk to us sympathetically. We don't need sympathy. We need courage to rebuild our lives.'

It was mid-March. Schools had been shut for over six weeks and nobody knew when they would reopen. How would the education process restart? The children in the camp realised that they had time on their hands even if they did not have books and pens. So they picked up a slate, got a piece of chalk and started teaching each other. The eighteen-year-olds taught the sixteen-year-olds, who in turn taught the twelve-year-olds. That was their spirit and zeal to survive.

Although houses had been wrecked, many fields were intact. In the afternoons, the youngsters were keen on taking us to their fields of flowers—the wadis. Our walks in the lush green fields were refreshing. I had read that these were arid areas prone to droughts, but here you could see the impact of irrigation technology.

One day, a young girl named Rubina decided to take us to her village to show us her house. She was so excited that, despite being tired from all our teaching and social commitments, we could not refuse her. The forty-five-minute walk felt like a hike through a hilly terrain, looking down on valleys—a mound of rubble formed the hill, while the empty spaces where houses had existed became the valley. The mound had been created when debris was being removed in search of people. It would take months to clear.

The young girl excitedly took us through all this. Then, as if looking at a scenic valley below, she pointed towards her 'house'—where the living room had been, her bedroom, the location of her study table, the back door into the fields. Her house was not a palace, but it was hers and she was giving us a tour with a sense of pride, or should I say, self-respect. I was dumbfounded. She was chirping happily about her memories in her house, but I was shattered as all we saw of the house were the tiles on the floor and 6 to 8 inches of light green wall demarcating where the rooms had once stood. All the houses in the neighbourhood were in a similar state.

This used to be her house, now reduced to memories, which would soon fade. But the trauma of loss would remain. Or would they be able to erase that too? Her house could not possibly be rebuilt the way it had been. Removing the rubble itself would take months. Our walk back to the camp was filled with silence and deep introspection.

What exactly is ours? We spend years building up and creating a false sense of 'mine' and pride in it, but does it really matter? It was something serious to ponder about. At that point, I did not know whether I was in a state of 'smashan vairagya'—the transient sense of detachment from materialism one feels in a cremation ground, the realisation that name, fame, money are all futile. This visit did hit me hard, as it must have many others, and left an impact on me for a while.

We returned for the evening classes which were no longer stressful for any of us. We had people of all ages, but mainly youngsters and a few people in their thirties or early forties. There was only one woman in her sixties. She remains fresh in my memory. She used to wear a blue bandhani sari and would cover her head with the pallu. The children would make fun of her. They had an inside joke—they kept saying that she was from Pakistan. Then one day she told us that she *had* come from Pakistan, to visit her relatives, and got stuck because of the earthquake. Now she could stay back since nobody else had any documents either. I never figured out whether she actually was an illegal immigrant or merely a visitor from another village. What really struck me was what she said about yoga. She said that many philosophers, doctors and psychologists who had lectured them in the past month had been trying to teach them to cope, saying that the trauma was transient and they had to bear it. She laughed and said, 'Of course, we have to bear it. We do not need lectures to understand that. We have no choice. But you are the first people who have shown us the means to bear it. The way we did the yogasanas have given us an insight into our aches and pains. But more than that, they have given us some calmness in the mind.'

It was gratifying that we had served our purpose. My mind was relieved. We would have the five batches that we had planned on paper.

The organisers wanted us to travel beyond the camp. They planned a visit to Anjar, a place famous for its metalwork, including knives and nutcrackers. We too were happy to leave the camp for a bit, our home for many days. A car took us to Anjar—it looked and felt eerie. We walked through a long, deserted, heavily dug up street. The ruins of shops stood on either side. This was the street where 420 schoolchildren were marching with the Indian flag on Republic Day when they heard a loud sound. The teachers thought it was a bomb and asked the children to lie down on the ground. Within seconds, the buildings lining the street collapsed and buried the children. A tragedy that, for us, justified the eerie atmosphere. We were walking on a street where 420 children had been killed in a fraction of a second. Was it an error of judgement on the part of the teachers? Would some have escaped if they were on their feet? Or was their fate written and nothing would have made any difference? Did the ones who had skipped the march, or were not selected for it, have better luck? It reminded me that in the Ramayana, Sita too had been engulfed by Mother Earth.

We then went to a shop that sold savouries, which were supposed to be a treat for the taste buds after our simple daily fare in the camp—khichdi, vegetables and many a soothing glass of buttermilk in the afternoons. But the taste of the savouries did not matter anymore. We were happy to get back to the camp and to our tents.

Seeing the response that our sessions got from the people in the camp, and the warmth we shared with them, the organisers decided that we should also visit the neighbouring Sungra village.

The destruction in Sungra was immense. The number of lives lost was much more than in Nagalpur, and many of the children had their arms and legs in casts. We were taken to a makeshift school where classes were held under a tin shed, for around fifty children. It was quiet as we waited for the kids to come in. Then we realised that they were all sitting in the neighbouring room, silent, with a blank look on their faces, though there was not a single adult in the room. Nothing can be more disturbing than a room full of silent twelve-year-olds.

Bhuj was a huge city in comparison, and there were many camps there, some run by the Swaminarayan group only for Hindus. Many may question segregating people into camps on the basis of religion. I too would have said the same sitting in the comfort of my home. But at that camp, I again realised that idealism was not reality. It made much more sense to have separate camps for people with different religious beliefs and related food habits. In times of such trauma, everyone is sensitive and differences in faith or food habits could hurt their sensibilities.

It was soon time for us to leave. The second batch of volunteers was to arrive shortly and we were to spend two days together. Our new friends in the camp were sad to see us go and so were we. We had gone there to teach them but we were leaving having learnt so much more about life from them.

It is easy to talk about living in the present, being happy in what we have, being tolerant to adversities. It is easy to say that all difficulties in life are transient, that we all have an inherent ability to handle problems. But it is something else to experience it. Guruji often said that need and greed are separated by a fine line. There, it appeared that all our 'needs' in life were actually 'greed'.

It was time to say our goodbyes. A girl came to us and confided, 'Can I share something with you? Don't feel bad about it, but when you came to the camp, the kind of clothes you had worn made us believe that you had come from some other camp. We felt sympathetic for you.' We were thankful to Guruji and his foresight. We would never have thought about this.

We returned home enriched. I started to write about my experience for the next issue of our magazine which was scheduled to release on Hanuman Jayanti. I had crossed the deadline but the printer was very considerate. He believed that we had done 'noble work'.

I was nearly finished with the magazine—the articles were ready, formatted and proofed and I just needed to put in the numbers to the table of contents. I informed our printer that I would email the PDF of the magazine in an hour, giving myself a grace period of half an hour. I saved the file frequently and made back-up copies on the laptop for emergency.

But as luck would have it, my five-year-old nephew came running in and boom!—my laptop was on the floor.

It would just not restart. My heart skipped many beats. What could I do? Should I have taken multiple back-ups on a pen drive or a CD? I would have done it after thirty minutes anyway, but now what could I do? My family was shaken but I became practical. I called up the laptop company. They said it could not be fixed in a week, let alone a day. What next? I could go back and search for the last few documents that were stored, then re-edit, format and proof them and the magazine would be ready.

Was it I who was so calm? Indeed, after spending about ten days with people who had lost everything, I had a fresh perspective. What had I lost? Just a few pages which could be rewritten.

We had started on the premise that we were going to help the 'unfortunate' victims of the earthquake, but there was a lot that I learnt in the process. I learnt that we may believe that we are helping somebody, but we don't do things for anybody except ourselves. We do things because we want to, either for pleasure or for an ego boost. I also learnt that a good teacher needs to go to the level of the students; a good therapist needs to feel the pain of the patient—to truly help them, we need to become them! I learnt however great we may be, or we think we are, we need to earn respect. We cannot demand it, for our claims at greatness mean nothing to anybody. It is easy to sit on a platform and talk about philosophy—it may make us appear learned, but that feel-good element is transient.

What has remained with me are the old 'Pakistani' woman's words—that we were the first to show them the *means* to bear their pain.

Sense-less or Super-senses?

What you are born with is God's gift to you; what you make of yourself is your gift to God.

–B.K.S. Iyengar

The concepts of necessity, comfort and luxury during my youth are so contrasting to the same concepts today. What was super-luxury in my youth is a basic necessity today. To use the cliché, change is constant. But sometimes change seems to be cyclical. It is like going full circle, coming back where we started, but with more wisdom.

Although we feel that we are progressing with the coming of the internet where information is at our fingertips, I sometimes feel that it is also taking us around full circle. With the internet, the means and the manner in which we communicate is changing. The elaborate written word is being substituted by initialisms, visuals and emojis. We may say the same thing that our ancestors said, but in all likelihood what may be perceived may differ.

Let us look at the three fairly popular emojis of a monkey covering its eyes, another covering its ears and a third covering its mouth. We grew up learning that these were Mahatma Gandhi's three wise monkeys, who were meant to teach us to 'see no evil, hear no evil and speak no evil'. These monkeys are also a part of Japanese maxims. Mizaru sees no evil, Kikazaru hears no evil and Ikazaru speaks no evil.

But what do people who use these emojis today wish to convey? The Mizaru emoji today conveys disbelief, laughter or 'I can't see such things'. Kikazaru covers his ears to express, 'I have not heard this, unbelievable!' While Ikazaru says, 'Oops, I should not have said that', or 'my lips are sealed—I know it but I will not say it'.

These three monkeys made me realise that they meant different things to different people at different points of time. Real communication is not just about what you say but what is perceived at the other end. Confusion, problems and issues arise when what is intended to be conveyed does not match what is perceived. Most relationship issues between people or nations can be due to this imbalance.

Mahatma Gandhi's wise monkey Bapu told us that we should close our eyes and not see anything evil, so that we don't get corrupted and influenced; Ketan said that we should not engage in loose talk and we should be careful in the choice of our words so that we don't hurt anybody, and Bandar said we should not listen to gossip or anything that can disturb us, lest we react. This is what I had understood.

But were the three wise monkeys actually telling me this? It is nice to close our eyes and ears to what is happening around us so that we don't get influenced by them. I definitely appreciate that, but I wonder how easy it is to remain unaffected by the environment. After all, we are social creatures, continuously influenced by what s around us. Can we live by isolating ourselves? Is that even possible?

Had I really understood what the wise monkeys were conveying? Were they asking me to cut myself off from the external 'bad' environment, or were they telling me to develop the strength to stand my ground irrespective of the influence of the environment? What I perceive makes a world of difference. As a child, I have to keep away from bad influences, but as I grow up, I need to develop my innate strength of not getting influenced.

As life progresses, I feel that maybe the monkeys were conveying something much deeper—getting into a state of deep meditation where our senses are 'cut off' from the environment and where nothing bothers us as we are in our inner world. This is the domain of yogis and saints—the statue of the Jain saint Gomateshwara Bahubali symbolises how deep in meditation he was, standing for twelve years, unaware of the creepers growing around his legs.

But, on the other hand, if I were to objectively look at these wise monkeys—what would life be if the eyes could not see, the ears did not hear and the tongue could not speak? What if three of the five common senses did not exist or existed barely? It is far beyond my imagination. I had seen people who were blind and noticed that often deaf people could not speak. But the lack of all three senses in a single individual was difficult to imagine. And I had no intentions to let my imagination go in that direction, as it seemed like a nightmare. This chapter was closed, or so I thought, till I landed in Israel in 2005.

Israel, the beautiful promised land where three religions share some of the most important historical places, is a small country. My Israeli friends joked it could be covered in a single day's drive. Deserts, lush green mountains, the Mediterranean and the Dead Sea were all packed into this small country.

I was enjoying the drives around the country until my hosts and friends Sara Tal and Kuka Shviro informed me that they had to return to Tel Aviv soon as they had a class for their deaf, dumb and blind students. Had I heard them correctly?

'Do you mean to say that you are going to teach deaf, dumb and blind people?'

They said, 'Yes.'

'But how do you do that? How do you communicate? Do you demonstrate to the deaf and orally instruct the blind?'

'No. They do not have sight or barely any sight and they cannot hear or speak.'

That hit me hard. We teach yoga by demonstrating the asanas and giving instructions to guide the students. I kept nagging them, 'How? If they cannot hear or see, how do you communicate?'

Instead of wasting their energy explaining, they asked me to join them and see for myself in their meeting with this group. It would be followed by a yoga class. I spontaneously agreed. But now my mind was totally distracted from the natural beauty around us. While I was curious about the class, I was gloomy and fearful and my heart was beating fast. To make me feel better, they told me that some of the fortunate ones had a little bit of their senses—maybe a little vision.

I became silent. Not out of a calm meditativeness, but at the thought of what I would be seeing in a few minutes. How awful to have all your major senses snatched away from you! How depressing it must be to not be able to communicate. How unhappy these people must be. My mind was in turmoil. I questioned my hosts, but all they said was, 'Please have patience. We will reach there soon.' But I was apprehensive and gloomy. Did I really want to meet such a group?

I had no choice as we had reached our destination, a coffee house. We walked through the café to a room at the back. There were about twenty middle-aged men and women in it, all smiling broadly, greeting and embracing each other. It looked like a reunion party of long-lost friends elated to meet each other. My mind raced. Had we reached the hall early? Perhaps the earlier event was not yet over? Or had we dropped in at another place before going to the meeting? Sara and Kuka were busy chatting with the people in the room. And my eyes were searching for the sad, unfortunate souls about whom I had been told. Then Sara introduced me to the head of the group. So we were at the right place. But where were the people who were lacking the faculties of vision and hearing?

Realising I was at a loss for words, Kuka decided to clear my doubts. She informed me that half the people there were students, and the other half interpreters. Each student had a personal interpreter who would explain to them the proceedings of the meeting.

The twenty people wore black t-shirts on which was written in a zigzag typeface, 'light is heard'. They sat in a circle, each student next to their interpreter. As the meeting progressed, the interpreters 'wrote' on the forearms of the students. It was through their hands that they did most of the communication. The interpreters moved their hands or took the hands of the students on to their own. The dialogue continued, and from far, it was very difficult to distinguish the interpreter from the student.

They were talking about the play that they had performed. Sara's sister-in-law was into theatre and had introduced the group to it. They had performed on stage and had even made a trip to Switzerland with their play. Each student reported on their recent experiences via the interpreter who spoke aloud in Hebrew, which Sara translated into English for me. Then, I realised that the sign language of each interpreter also differed. The commonality in this group was that they were currently in Israel. But they had originated from different countries. Some individuals had emigrated from Russia and spoke a different language. This meant nearly three tiers of translations/interpretations.

My eyes opened wider still. It made me see life in terms of the motivational adage so often repeated by my schoolteachers—where there is a will there is a way. After decades I 'saw' the meaning of this statement.

There was no sign of gloom, unhappiness or resentment on any face. They were an expressive, cheerful, chirpy and smiling lot. I realised that when others don't have what we have, we think they are unhappy. For instance, we might feel sorry for people who belong to a lower economic strata than ours. If we hear of somebody staying in a chawl rather than in a luxurious apartment, we sympathise with them as if they are unhappy. But what if we changed our perception to realise that those living in a chawl could have a larger extended family as compared to those who have the freedom of privacy. Happiness is a state of mind, which has nothing to do with what we don't have and everything to do with appreciating what we do have. These 'unfortunate' people without sight or speech were happy.

After the meeting, I was introduced to many of them. All were eager to know where I came from. The interpreters took their forefingers and placed it on the middle of their foreheads between their eyebrows—it meant the bindi, which represented India. Israelis seem to love Indians and these people were no different. They were genuinely happy to meet me and greeted me warmly by holding my hand.

One of the students, who looked like a model in her smart clothes, high heels and painted lips and nails, asked through her interpreter why I was so thin. Taken aback, I asked Sara whether she was really blind. She had been walking around the room confidently in her heels, which I would never have managed. It was unbelievable! When the eyes and ears both don't function, it is so difficult to have a good sense of balance. Yet, here she was, walking around in full confidence in those heels. Was she really not able to see or hear? Yes! She was really not able to see or hear. Everything looked so 'normal'. How did they manage it?

I was introduced to the other members. They touched my hands to identify me in the way we look at faces to recognise people. How does one generate a memory from a sense of touch? The introduction was not just a formality, some were interested in finding out more about me. They were told that I had come to Israel for a yoga convention. One of them asked me a question with his hands. I do not know sign language, so I needed my interpreter to understand what he was saying. But before I could orally answer, the man opened his bag and brought out a chart with English and Braille alphabets adjacent to each other. I was expected to answer in Braille. Imagine saying a sentence in extremely slow motion. Even for a simple answer like 'I come from Mumbai, India,' I had to break up the sentence into words and words into letters and then move his finger over each corresponding Braille letter. It was indeed a great test of patience.

Of course, since I did not know Braille, it was difficult for me. But it wasn't easy for them either. Imagine formulating each word character by character, then making the sentence and finally combining all to understand my response. The link between letters while making even simple sentences could easily be lost. I admire the patience and motivation of the visually impaired to read entire books in Braille! This young man was very well read about India. He had never been to the country, but was interested in visiting.

How important is patience! We can learn anything, achieve anything, acquire anything, but do we have the patience, perseverance and enthusiasm to do so? I had entered the hall with the preconceived notion of meeting unhappy blind, deaf and mute people. But they actually opened my eyes!

After the meeting, it was time for the yoga class. By this time, I was overwhelmed. The mats were spread out and the students were made to stand on the edge of the mat with their interpreters standing behind. Sara started her instructions and the interpreters communicated it to the students. They went through many asanas like Tadasana, Urdhva Hastasana, Utthita Trikonasana and Supta Padangushthasana with relative ease. Sara would instruct in Hebrew and the interpreters would get them to adjust their pose. It reminded me of my own teaching experiences. We give instructions; if they are not clear, we call the students and demonstrate. And if their eyes and ears still cannot grasp what is being said, we physically correct the students. This is exactly how these students were taught, totally through sensations and feelings. They utilised the sense of touch to the maximum and indeed had greater sensitivity then most 'normal' people. Their sense of alignment and balance was so internal that it reflected in the way they performed their asanas.

All the apprehensions I'd had before the start of the class vanished. I felt so much a part of the class and the teaching process that, involuntarily, I wanted to guide and correct. They were like any other yoga students. In fact, they were more yogic in their practices than I was. My mind would sometimes wander when I practised, but theirs did not.

Guruji has often referred to the internal mind and the external mind. The external mind is directed outwards by the senses. And as the mind travels in the 'outside' world, we feel it is out of control. We talk about the mind wandering and not being focussed. But a yogic mind is not distracted by the senses; the senses take a U-turn and move inwards, away from sensual gratification outside, and spread within our own self, taking us into a state of deep meditation.

This is what Gandhiji's wise monkeys now imply to me. It is neither closing the eyes and the senses to the world nor being unaffected by the pressures of the world. It is about going deep within to see the truth—the existence of the Supreme within us. Here, these students whose senses were supposedly impaired, were in fact much more focussed and yogic in their approach to yoga—like the symbolic Kurmasana where, similar to a tortoise withdrawing into its shell, we draw all our senses inwards. These students were more involved and far more evolved than I could have imagined!

Due to time constraints, the class ended earlier than scheduled, as they were now to be treated to a slide show about their trip to Switzerland.

Before I met them, I had felt sympathetic towards them—I would even say I pitied them, thinking of them as 'poor things'. But now I realised that there was no need for sympathy. They were just different and spoke a different language.

I had reached the pinnacle of my imagination about how they functioned. A few hours ago, it was difficult for me to believe the way they moved and socialised, then there was the yoga class and now they were going to 'watch' a slide show on a big screen.

I understood why neither Sara nor Kuka explained to me how they taught these people. Words could never do justice to the experience. While I waited for the show, I sat with Kuka and Sara and enquired about how all this started.

I was told most of these people had a rare genetic disorder. There were even two sisters in the group—one of them the immaculately dressed lady. The little sensory perception they had at birth had weakened over time, and the only way they could feel was through touch and vibrations caused by people's movements around them. Sara told me that I had not been too wrong in assuming they would be unhappy. They had indeed been depressed, imprisoned within the confines of their homes, isolated and without any interactions with anybody. Outings were rare. Their self-confidence was totally lacking. All they received was sympathy. They were alive but not living. What could one expect in such conditions?

It was then that they were introduced to theatre by Sara's sister-in-law and yoga by Sara. In two years, they were living a vibrant life, possibly much more vibrant than even a person with so-called 'normal' senses. The transition was gradual but remarkable. Isolation turned into socialisation, depression changed into cheerfulness, pale gloomy faces now showed exuberance. Nothing hindered their lives now. Two of the students had even fallen in love with each other. It was incredible to think these people had emotionally been anything other than how they appeared now. They were happy and so were their friends and families! They were content.

Contentment was the word. They were happy with what they got and everything else only made them happier. There were no expectations. It is expectations from oneself and others that breeds discontent. We believe that success comes with challenges. So people are constantly challenged to do more, achieve more, earn more, display more—but what has that got to do with happiness? These people got their fortunate first break to get out of their lives of gloom. That gave them happiness and after that everything else was a bonus.

The well-read young man who tested my patience with Braille told me that he was indeed happy that he was not distracted by external sounds and sights and enjoyed his inner sound. How profound! They had no complaints, so satisfied were they with what they had. Nor did they live in a world of illusion, imagining what they did not have. They had beautifully adapted to what they had.

Adaptation. The more we can adapt, life becomes pleasant. We believe that we are happier when we have more, when we have choices, when we take our own decisions. We want to live life in an organised manner where everything is meticulously planned and executed. Good organisational skills are excellent, but is it not equally important to have an ability to handle things when they don't go as planned? With excellent organisational set-ups and well-defined standard operating protocols, do we tend to lose our adaptability—something we Indians used to be good at, jugaad? I am not implying that we should not have standard operating protocols in our workplaces. We should. But would it not be exciting to at least have mental exercises around handling sudden and unforeseen situations?

I had got my lessons for the day—patience, perseverance, enthusiasm, contentment and now adaptation. What more could I learn from these 'poor' souls, as I had imagined them to be?

The group was so excited to 'see' and 'hear' the slides of their recent trip to Switzerland. Again, the interpreters communicated who was on the screen and what he/she was doing—fooling around with friends or sliding on the snow. They were like a bunch of happy children, excited, teasing each other, fighting playfully, laughing and enjoying themselves.

It was like a normal scene after a trip, when we share memories with others through slides, photos and videos. I sat in a corner, and rather than look at the screen, watched these people—an unforgettable scene that gave me goosebumps.

It was time to wind up. Goodbyes were being said. Volunteers would drive back home these artists who came from different parts of the city, and in a couple of cases, even another city altogether.

I waited for my hosts to drive me back to my hotel, processing all that I had just witnessed. While the interpreters were having a discussion amongst themselves, a student was quietly relaxing on a few cushions, waiting for somebody to give her a lift back home. She would suddenly make some sounds and smile. I found it strange. Then I realised that she reacted like that whenever somebody passed by. I could feel no vibration or sound, but she could. As someone walked on the floor, the vibration generated was transmitted to her cushions and she felt it. I was flabbergasted. I would not have believed it if somebody had told me this, but I had seen it with my own eyes.

Should I say then that they were deprived of senses? Or should I say that they had super-senses?

Living with Something Extra

Purity is when there is no anxiety, no worry, no thinking.

–B.K.S. Iyengar

We are what we are because of the genes present in each of our cells. These genes are neatly organised into small packages called chromosomes. We have twenty-three pairs of chromosomes, each having a very specific role. We inherit one set from each parent. During the early stages of fetal development, there is an exchange between these pairs; we develop our own set of chromosomes that give us our identity—our appearance, our physical and mental functions and our behaviour. What happens when we have an extra chromosome? What if one chromosome has three copies rather than two?

Medically, this condition of having an abnormal number of chromosomes is called aneuploidy. One such condition, where the body has a third copy of chromosome 21, or a part of it, is Down's syndrome. Parents may realise it during the pregnancy itself if the chromosomes of the chorionic villi are tested. Or when the baby is born, they can gather this from the baby's slightly different facial features. The chromosomal analysis confirms it.

The lives of new parents does change after the arrival of a baby. There is joy when the infant crosses milestone after milestone and there is fatigue from running after the toddler. If these milestones are not touched at the right time, it could bring on a whole range of stressful emotions. After reality is accepted, life becomes all about accepting that this member in the family is different and bring up the child accordingly.

Then comes the fear of the future. How would the child live once he or she grows up? Fortunately, there are organisations that work towards empowering adults with different skills.

We were approached by an organisation called Anchorage, which worked with differently abled adults; they wanted our assistance in teaching yoga. My sister Arti, who has had a lot of experience teaching children with special needs, joined me on our first visit to this organisation.

All we knew when we entered Anchorage was that it trained differently abled adults to perform jobs that would not only keep them occupied but also give them a livelihood.

We saw that all the trainees were deeply engrossed in fixing sockets. Anchorage taught them to assemble electrical switches and plugs, refinish imitation jewellery, assemble pens, prepare paper bags, label envelopes for conferences and put together housekeeping kits of shampoos, soaps, conditioners and moisturisers for the hospitality industry. What may appear mundane to some was done in all sincerity by this group.

They were overtly friendly but to speak the truth, we were really nervous. We had not met many differently abled adults in our life. But once the classes started, we realised that they just saw and understood things differently from us.

It was decided that Arti, relatively more experienced than the rest of us, would teach them.

Like with any new group of students, the class started with Tadasana—where we stand straight and tall. The teacher stood in Tadasana in the front and the students were expected to follow. We did not expect them to follow all the oral instructions, but unlike in the regular classes, where the students see the teacher as a 'mirror' and visually imitate him or her, these students imitated the teacher in totality. They did exactly what their teacher did and said. They stood exactly like the teacher, which meant, they were standing with their backs to the teacher! How could we teach if the students didn't face us?

We, so-called 'normal' people, face our teacher and attempt to become a 'mirror image' of our teacher. Even in life, we create images of ourselves, sometimes so many that we forget the real us and tend to live in a make-believe world. The purpose of yoga is to remove all these veils and see the truth as it is. I wondered whether these 'special' adults were seeing the truth as it is. No biases, no distortions, no impressions, just the truth.

When the teacher pointed to herself and asked them to look at her, they looked in all possible directions. They possibly understood that they had to do something with their eyes on the external front. That was still some progress—they were at least facing the teacher! They did not differentiate between the subject and the object. They became one with the object. That's why in our first meeting, when they were assembling switches, they appeared so engrossed in their work. I had mistakenly thought that the work required their total absorption. But, in hindsight, I know they were absorbed because they became one with the task in their hands. They were not doing anything—they were in it. Was my imagination going wild? Would it be too far-fetched to say that they were totally absorbed—just what is expected of a yoga practitioner?

The teacher then physically showed them her foot and asked them to look at her foot. They looked at her face, that too for a fraction of a second. She realised that there was no coordination between what they were looking at, and what she was showing them. Their minds registered neither her words nor her actions. How would she communicate with them?

They had little coordination between the legs and the eyes either. But then how many of us even realise that a tremendous coordination exists between our legs and our state of mind? If our legs are bent at the knees, we slouch and the mind is dull. We might believe we are meditating, but our spine is not straight when we and our mind is wandering. We too don't have coordination!

Guruji asserted that actions speak louder than words, but that would be true in this case only if Arti could get them to 'see' her, and her actions. She then remembered Guruji's quote, 'The eyes are the windows to the brain.' She told them that she wanted them to open their eyes wide. After all, their eyes were their subject as well as their object. And lo and behold! They did look at her feet and theirs.

Then she asked them to spread their legs for the standing asanas. They spread their feet only a foot apart. If she asked them to spread their feet further, they did so only by half an inch. That was it! Fear is universal. When we venture into new asanas or unknown zones, we too become extra-cautious. Except that words console us, give us confidence and we progress a little faster. In their case, it was very difficult to win their confidence and that was a test of patience for the teacher.

The class carried on. Next came Utthita Trikonasana, where we turn the left foot slightly in, turn the right leg ninety degrees outwards and then take the right arm down towards the right foot. This was a real challenge for the teacher. For the students, it was difficult to grasp. Any amount of explanation and demonstration was futile. So the teacher went to each of them and turned their foot. There was a lot of resistance from their body—the leg would immediately bounce back to the earlier position like a spring. Aren't we 'normal' people also creatures of habit and find it difficult or sometimes impossible to forgo a habit—whether smoking or the morning tea or even slouching? I started seeing 'ourselves', the so-called 'normal' people, in them. We don't see any faults in our behaviour, but we label them so easily.

The teacher also noticed that the students tended to drop their heads to the side, as if one side was heavier. Another thing that she noticed was that most of them saw things exactly opposite to what was said and shown. If she showed them straight legs, they would say that those were bent and would bend their legs for asanas with straight legs. If she bent forward in Adho Mukha Virasana, they would lie flat on their stomach with the legs straight. If she did Supta Baddha Konasana, they would lie back like in Shavasana. It was as if their brain registered straight as bent and bent as straight. They saw the elbow as the knee and the knee as the elbow. On the neurological front, we did not know why they did the opposite of what was shown or why they saw it that way. And all of them showed similar behaviour.

It was difficult to get any verbal feedback from them as only a few of them spoke. For quite some time, the teacher was under the impression that one of the students could not speak since the only responses he gave were in grunts. It must be frustrating not to be able to express thoughts in words. Imagine being in a foreign land where you do not know the language and are unable to communicate—how aggravating it can be. We realised why they threw temper tantrums. No, 'tantrums' seems a harsh word—those were possibly their expressions of frustration with people not understanding them.

But what was unique about them was their enthusiasm. There was a tall and lean young man with a very stiff body. He communicated only with gestures that his mother alone could understand. He attempted everything the teacher made them do but with tears in his eyes—tears because of the tremendous pain that he must have been experiencing due to his stiffness. But the touching part was that he seemed to experience something beyond the pain—a sense of achievement, a sense of being able to go beyond his limitations. One day his mother came to the teacher with tears of joy in her eyes. She said that her son always tried to repeat at home what he had learnt in class and showed it to the entire family. The satisfaction that he got from his progress reflected in his sound sleep, which meant sound sleep for the mother too.

As the teacher started understanding their behaviour, she started modifying her method of teaching. If she wanted them to listen to her, follow her, then she had to speak their language. She needed to communicate in a manner that they would understand. For that, she had to understand them. This is a lesson for all teachers. The job of a teacher is to go to the level of the students and raise them up instead of showing off their own knowledge.

The question now was how to communicate with them. If she wanted to tell them that their legs had to be straight, then she not only needed to communicate what 'straight' was, but also what 'legs' were. Their eyes did not seem to be bothered about what was outside of them. So the teacher did Uttanasana. 'These are the legs.' The next question that they were asked was 'Are they straight?' There was no reply. But if the question was 'Are they straight or bent?', the instant reply was 'bent'. It was now clear that they did 'see' things, but what they saw was the opposite of what we did. They could also not respond to open-ended questions. But if the questions meant making a choice between two options, then they could respond.

These were the means to reach out to them, but communication would be possible only if we could learn their language rather than trying to teach them ours. Our purpose was to teach yoga and not language after all.

Thus the process of learning started. The teacher did Uttanasana and asked them, 'What are the legs doing?' They promptly replied that the legs were standing. So when the teacher asked them to keep the legs standing, the legs became straight!

For Urdhva Hastasana, where they had to take both the arms over the head, asking them to straighten the arms or 'bend the arms' also did not work. Their hands would go up very lazily. There was either no life in their arms or they did not understand what it meant to lift and extend them. So the instruction was 'Clap loudly over the head.' That brought some life into their arms and in their own selves. They were alert and all smiles! The claps were an acknowledgement to their own selves. They were happy and so was their teacher. She was learning the art of communicating with them.

If we required them to critically observe us to learn, then learning their language too required us to critically observe their behaviour. Let us take the example of Viparita Dandasana with the support of a chair. We sit on the chair by inserting the legs in the space between the seat of the chair and the back rest and then sliding forward and resting the back on the seat of the chair. To come out of this asana, we hold the side legs of the chair, lift the chest up and then take the legs out of the chair. Some of the students tried to slide down through the gap between the seat and the backrest of the chair and slip down onto the floor. They were just not ready to take their feet off the floor! Interestingly, having taught thousands of people over the years, I have not seen any adult get out of the chair in that fashion. And if I asked them to, it would be a big challenge. These students just did things unconventionally, not as a revolt but naturally.

Now that their cooperation had improved because of better communication, what was required was motivation — to take up a little more complex asanas. Talking was definitely not expected to work. So they played a game. The teacher would demonstrate an asana and then ask one of the students to 'play' the teacher on stage. The change in roles motivated them and each of them wanted to play the teacher. They were soon imitating the teacher. This motivated the rest to be on the platform and 'lead'. And a phone call from the Anchorage office motivated the teacher in turn. The person on the other side informed us that the students had expressed that they were enjoying the yoga and were looking forward to the classes. One should not forget that these students spoke nothing but the truth.

Geetaji had advised us to restrict the use of props for this group, especially in the beginning. Any kind of touch would be distracting. The props would help but they needed to befriend the prop first.

Take the example of Supta Baddha Konasana. We sit straight with our legs bent at the knees and the feet touching each other. It is like doing namaskar with the feet. We sometimes place a yoga belt around the sacral region, then take it underneath the feet and tighten it and then lie on our back.

Even after multiple demonstrations, when asked to do Supta Baddha Konasana, they tended to go into the asana, place their belt around or near their feet and then just hold it.

They all feared going into Sarvangasana or Viparita Dandasana like most adults do when trying it for the very first time. The only difference was that their fear lasted much longer. Three of them would hold the chair very tightly and move closer to the back rest of the chair instead of away from it, which made it impossible for them to go into the pose. They would hold their breath and perspire and their eyes would harden when their neck was curved even slightly for the head to go back. How could we get them to curve back? They would immediately bounce up if they were made to curve backwards even slightly. After a few unsuccessful attempts, the teacher realised that they needed support to overcome their fear. She used innovation. She supported the back of their head with one end of a bolster placed vertically and then slowly lowered the bolster and along with that their head and trunk were brought down. Of course, this took a few attempts as the teacher first gave them confidence by just getting them to curve their neck and gradually increased the curvature. Fear needs support. Thus, the moment their head was on a support, it was possible for them to move.

For Sarvangasana, she continuously patted their dorsal spine, which guided them to descend that part of the body. This touch gave them a sense of security, and later they carried their bolster like toddlers do their security blanket! The bolster was their first friend and as soon as they came to class, they got their friend to be next to them. One of the students had a habit of assuring himself that he could do it and would say aloud: 'I am not scared now, I can do it, I will do it,' and he did!

Soon the students became friends with their teacher as well as with the props. They did not come out of compulsion but because they enjoyed the class. They were breaking barriers, getting more courageous and trying new things. This would surely help them to cope in life. These students also taught us a lot; some of the tricks we picked up while teaching them could also be used in our other classes—other adults have many child-like traits too!

Their innocence was like that of a child. Once, the teacher was in Shirshasana before the class had started. This was possibly the first time they had seen somebody upside down, and their innocence and curiosity made each one of them bend down to look into the teacher's face, feel her eyes and nose. They then reassured themselves and each other, 'This is our Arti Aunty.' Some of them would pull her cheeks gently or give her a gentle kiss on the cheek like you would to a child.

Of course we had to be extra-careful and not forget their normal ageing problems. Most of them were in the age group of thirty-five to fifty, but they seemed to have 'ageing' problems much earlier than 'normal' adults. Some of them were already suffering from heart ailments, joint stiffness and muscle atrophy in addition to other physiological problems.

When we talk of age, we only refer to the chronological age. But we humans have different kinds of age, including emotional, intellectual and physiological.

Although their mental age did not correspond to their chronological and physiological age, they were aware of their chronological age. They realised and felt insulted if people spoke to them or treated them as children. Unfortunately, many people tend to do just that. Would we like it if somebody treated us like infants? They knew they were adults and liked to be treated as such. They did not cooperate when spoken to like children. They responded by saying, 'I am not a child, I am thirty-five years old!'

The feedback from the staff and family members had been encouraging. Their posture had improved and along with that the feeling of depression seemed to have decreased. Yoga had improved the mobility of Ms A's shoulders and increased the flexibility in the joints in two men. Mr B did not wet his pants as frequently as earlier. Mr C now slept more regularly. The heart condition of

Ms D had improved and Mr E now made more eye contact. There was tremendous improvement in Mr F and he was much more alert and flexible than before. Overall, the quality of life seemed to have changed for the better. They loved their yoga class so much that they were on their best behaviour for a few days before each class since they knew that the punishment for misbehaviour was 'no yoga class'.

The smiles on their faces after the class and their gesture of joining the thumb with the index finger was enough to motivate the teachers.

My thoughts about these adults changed with time.

At the end of a year and a half, I wondered whether they were simply looking at things differently. And how our society treats people who are different! When travel was not so common, and foreigners were not seen in all corners of India, a white or a black man made heads turn. We looked up at the white man and down on the black man just because they were different from the majority.

These adults at Anchorage could not communicate in 'our' language but they did communicate—it was we who could not understand their means of communication. Do we then have the right to see them differently because their 'language' differed from those of the majority?

They understood words differently from us—for example, they seemed to confuse the knee for the elbow and vice versa. But perhaps they were not confused;

perhaps the words had just replaced each other in their mind's dictionary and so, similarly, 'straight' meant 'bent', and 'bent' meant 'straight' to them. What if straight legs were called standing legs? Can we not accept that the meaning of a word in our language is completely opposite in theirs? If I were to lecture in Marathi on the streets of Beijing, should I also be considered insane?

Some of them did not have the capacity to analyse and reason, nor did they have very fine motor skills. But then how many of us have the analytical, logical and intellectual capacity of a rocket scientist or a molecular biologist or the fine motor skills of a neurosurgeon? We too do not understand their language or possess their skills, but we look at them in awe. It is just that these adults are on the opposite end of the spectrum when it comes to such skills and capabilities while we are somewhere between. But does it really matter?

What was also remarkable about them was their complete lack of duplicity. They expressed what they felt. They had the innocence and purity of children, the stubbornness too. They wore no masks and had no facades. It could get embarrassing sometimes, but should we not accept the truth as it is? Why do we need to create an aura or image of ourselves and then live in that 'created' image? In this process, we move away from our true selves.

In fact, if we had the ability to see things as they are, without prejudice or judgement, there would be no issues between people and societies. If we have the ability to accept what we are rather than hide it, we will not be bothered by what people say. Of course, we need to be concerned about the society in which we live but not at the cost of moving away from our own reality. We want our children to be engineers or IAS officers because the society reveres these roles but we forget the desire of our own children, who may want to be primary school teachers or artists or musicians.

These adults were honest individuals who did things differently from the majority. But we have no right to label them. If we do so, the same label applies to all of us since most of us cannot even communicate in one-fourth of our own languages. We tend to express ourselves in the manner that the world would like to hear and appreciate. Their world permits them to be who they are.

Today, I look at these adults differently; rather, I respect them and all those who honestly work with them. For it is not easy to live in a world where you are unable to conform to the norms of 'normalcy'. There is something to learn from them.

Epilogue

Your body is your child, look after it!

–B.K.S. Iyengar

We all hope that we do not have to face the difficulties that Shirly, Birgit, Mark and the other people in my stories have experienced. But I hope that the beautiful manner in which they have handled their lives inspires readers as much as it inspired me.

There is a commonality in their approach: Accept whatever life has in store for you. Do not wallow in self-pity about your condition or situation, no matter what it is. Always remember that it is part of life and not bigger than life. Take small steps as they did, and life will not be as bad as it may seem.

Another common factor is that they were all practitioners of Iyengar Yoga.

Guruji B.K.S. Iyengar was born during the influenza pandemic of 1918. In fact, his mother suffered from influenza when she was pregnant with him. He was born a sickly child and was incidentally introduced to yoga by his brother-in-law so that he could gain freedom from his never-ending illnesses.

He latched on to the word 'health', and sincerely started his yoga practice. Day by day, over the decades, his practice revealed many aspects of health—of the body, mind, emotions, intelligence and conscience. Together, these lead to divine health or spiritual bliss. Having started life in a seemingly bottomless pit of continuous ill-health, he gradually surfaced to see life in full bloom. The experience gave him wisdom with which he could see the true self. A realised soul, he embarked on the process of uplifting humanity with the pillars of asana and pranayama which lead us to experience all the eight limbs of yoga.

The characters in my stories all practised yoga as taught in the tradition of Guruji, which supported their zest for life. If yoga could add on so much to their lives, can we imagine what it can do for our lives, which are not beset with the kind of issues theirs are?

I now share some practical hints and tips that were given by Guruji on how to withstand trauma, which is bound to be a part of our lives, wherever in the world we live, whether we are rich or poor.

Developing Strength to Withstand the Invaders

Imagine a visitor comes to your house unannounced and you are gracious enough to let him in. Unknown to you, he uses all your resources for his own development, creates his own family and invades your house. And you are left at the mercy of this visitor, or should I say, invader!

We cannot imagine such a situation. Of course, we would be alert enough to not let a visitor take over our abode in that way. We would use our own resources to get rid of him: we can cajole, use physical force or external strength like the police and the law. In doing so, we might sometimes land up in a fight and in the process injure ourselves.

It seems like wild imagination, not a real possibility. Why would we even wait for a situation where we have to damage our own selves to get rid of an invader?

Well, such invisible and unfriendly visitors to our abode are the viruses. So miniscule that over twenty million of them fit onto a pinhead. So tiny but so smart! All they need to do to survive is to cheat their way into our bodies and cells. Once they are in, our poor innocent cells treat them as their own and help them multiply. And how do they thank their hosts? By destroying them!

Today, it is the coronavirus pandemic which has frightened humans across countries. We can only hope that it gets regulated and does not reach the proportions of the 1918 influenza pandemic, then known as the Spanish flu. The 1918 influenza was called the Spanish flu not because it originated in Spain, but because that country reported a large number of infections. This flu infected five hundred million people worldwide, killing twenty to fifty million. And this was when people did not hop across the globe in a single day.

The flu is not something we bothered about much growing up. We got a fever, rested for a few days, let the systems of the body rest by eating less, and in a couple of days, we were back to normal. When somebody said that they had the flu, it wasn't a big deal. It was something common and everyone recovered. That is what people who have lived in the 1960s, 1970s and even the 1990s would have said. But in the last two-and-a-half decades, SARS, MERS, the swine flu or the H1N1 infections have frightened people across the world. Today's coronavirus infection or COVID-19 has literally destroyed the health of the world—not just of those afflicted but also of those who have not even been exposed. It has generated fear, and the genuine fear of its spread has led to locking down of towns and cities, affecting the world economy. It has led to physical, mental, emotional and economic destruction. Our cumulative human strength is not able to contain this virus which travels with total freedom, cutting across all our man-made boundaries!

As I mentioned earlier, Guruji was born during the influenza pandemic of 1918 and his mother was not spared the infection during her pregnancy. She survived, and so did her baby. But the outcome of the unhealthy pregnancy was that her son, Sundararaja, was born a sickly child. Children born in the early twentieth century were afflicted by many infectious diseases. Poverty led to malnutrition and poor immunity, and the absence of vaccines led to sickness and even death of children. To add to that, a child born sick did not have much hope. Sundararaja happened to be one of them. His childhood was plagued with ill health, which made attending school regularly difficult, ultimately leading to his poor formal education.

Call it God's grace on him or on the world, he was initiated into yoga by his brother-in-law who could not stand the sight of his wife's teenage brother being so sick. Sundararaja was taught a few asanas, which made him realise what the word 'health' possibly meant. He redefined it, and re-redefined it from his own experiences. It was no longer a disease-free state, nor was it merely a state of physical, mental and spiritual well-being as the World Health Organisation says. He redefined health as the state of well-being of the body, mind, emotions, intellect, consciousness, morality, sociality and conscience, which ultimately leads to a state of divine health. And thus he stayed with this subject and even merged with this subject of yoga till his last breath.

It is interesting that ill-health introduced him to yoga, and with yoga he gave health to millions across the world.

The Spanish flu had caused his ill-health, and ninety-one years later, in 2009, the swine flu caused by the H1N1 virus, infiltrated his karma bhumi, Pune. More than the flu itself, the fear of contracting it worried people. Travellers feared contracting it from the locals, while the locals feared that the visitors may have brought the virus with them.

During the 2009 swine flu epidemic, government authorities attempted to control the spread of the virus by closing down schools and institutions. RIMYI was also not spared and was asked to shut down for a week, although none of the students were affected. Pune was the epicentre of the epidemic in India, and with so many visitors from foreign lands at RIMYI, the risk appeared to be high. However, officials did not realise that RIMYI had a very potent mode of prevention of swine flu—Guruji's experience and wisdom.

We can curtail the spread of any infection by social isolation. But is that a real, practical solution? Why don't all the people exposed to an infected person acquire the disease? If an H1N1-infected person sneezes, they do release tonnes of the virus, and all the people who breathe that air should get infected. But that does not happen. Only a few contract the disease. And most people who get infected manage to recover without medication; only some develop complications. For most, a little rest enables them to get rid of the disease. The majority who suffer and who may die from the infection are those with already compromised health because of chronic conditions or age-related decline in immunity.

It is all about immunity. Build a strong immune system, and you reduce your risk of being susceptible to infections. But how do we do that?

Modern science is aware of the mechanisms of building muscles and the cardiovascular system through exercise, but not the immune system. Vitamins, a healthy diet and a hygienic lifestyle are supposed to help, but there does not seem to be anything at the moment that can specifically help build the immune system.

RIMYI did abide by the state government's orders. So when students—many of them from various countries who had booked their place at least two years in advance—came geared up for class and read on the notice board that classes were suspended for a week, they were disappointed. They did not want to stay cooped up in their hotel rooms or apartments, but they had no choice.

Guruji used to say, 'Convert disappointment into appointment.' He decided to give them a practice sequence for that week. The good thing about yoga is that it can be practised anywhere. All we need is a floor and a blanket or two, which all hotel rooms provide. The students went back with the means to spend time fruitfully in their rooms and, at the same time, with the wisdom on how to build their immunity, which would be handy throughout their life.

I believe that all the readers of this book would be happy with a practical solution or the practical wisdom of B.K.S. Iyengar. So I reproduce the advice that was given by Guruji then, which remains applicable now and for times to come. You can refer to the details on how to practise these asanas from the books *Light on Yoga*, *Yoga in Action: Preliminary Course* and *Yoga for Sports*. In case you are unable to do the classical asanas, *Yoga for Sports* provides all the details and variations on how to do them with the help of support. Start with the duration for which you are comfortable in doing these asanas and, with time, you will be able to stay longer in each of them.

Morning practice

- Uttanasana for 5 minutes
- Adho Mukha Svanasana for 5 minutes
- Prasarita Padottanasana for 3 minutes
- Shirshasana for 5 minutes straight and 10 minutes with variations
- Viparita Dandasana (on chair) for 5 minutes
- Sarvangasana for 10 minutes

- Halasana for 5 minutes
- Sarvangasana cycle for 5 minutes
- Setu Bandha Sarvangasana for 5 minutes
- Viparita Karani for 5 minutes
- Shavasana with Viloma / Ujjayi pranayama for 10 minutes

Evening practice

- Shirshasana for 10 minutes
- Sarvangasana for 10 minutes
- Halasana for 5 minutes
- Setu Bandha Sarvangasana for 10 minutes
- Shavasana with Viloma / Ujjayi pranayama for 10 minutes

Please note that this is not a prescription that would prevent illness, but it will surely build your ability to withstand illnesses.

Coping with Trauma

We don't really know where the word 'date' originates from or the history of its use but history and dates go hand in hand. And some dates remain etched in our memory for life. One such date is 11 September. A date that changed the lives of people all over the world or should I say the face of this world.

I still remember receiving a phone call from my cousin late in the evening of 9/11. 'Switch on the TV.' There was a great sense of urgency in his voice. When I switched on the TV, the image on it was unimaginable. What was I seeing? An animation sequence? Science fiction? A plane ramming into buildings! How could that be possible? How could any pilot lose his judgement to that extent? And in case something was wrong with the pilot, was there not a co-pilot? Then there was a shot of another aircraft doing the same thing at another location. It was an unimaginable scene. Even the worst nightmare in the world could not have imitated that visual.

What happened later is etched in the pages of history. In the immediate future, there was tremendous fear at multiple levels. The families of the three thousand killed were in a state of shock. Those injured and their friends and families were recovering from the shock but living under fear and uncertainty—how debilitating would their condition be and what would life have in store? Losing limbs or the senses or becoming dependent on others—these are not things that are easy to live with. There was also the fear of retaliation at the individual level: South Asians were being taunted or even killed.

And there was mass fear that this could happen again. Who would be the target? It could be anybody. The fear was spreading.

The fact that the targets were innocent people made matters worse. They were not on a battle field, they were people with families—with young children, old parents, newlyweds—it was just about anybody. It could have been you or me! Life can be so uncertain.

I would not like to delve into this history. It has been widely written about and analysed by politicians, historians, psychologists and many others. But as an ordinary individual, I was concerned about my friends and fellow yoga practitioners in New York. I wrote to my friend Bobby Clennell, enquiring about her, her family, her studio, her students and the rest of the teachers. She informed me that there was an apparent fear in the air not only in New York but in all the major cities.

This fear was genuine and not generated by social media, which did not exist then. Having returned from Kutch a few months ago, I could relate to the fear of the unknown that each citizen was facing—whether they were a victim or they were someone misunderstood by people as representative of the community held responsible for the attack or they were someone in fear of a repeat attack.

I sympathised with them, but except for a few consoling words, what more could I do? I didn't know whether those words could help practically. The memories of the past would linger on and fear of the future would hang like a sword—would this happen again? It reminded me of a story that I had heard in childhood about a man and his shoes.

It was a story of two neighbours in an apartment building. The young man who lived on the higher floor would come in late every night. And then he would remove his shoes and dump them on the floor, which would disturb his old neighbour downstairs. The first thud would awaken the old man and the next would ruin his sleep. This went on for days. Then the old man decided to have a word with him. That night, out of habit, the young man threw the first shoe, which again awakened the old man. Then the young man suddenly remembered his conversation with the old man and quietly placed the other shoe down. The old man, however, waited for the second thud. He waited and waited and waited but it did not come. The waiting turned out to be worse than the actual disturbance.

As much as we did not want another terrorist attack in any part of the world, the fear of one happening was as bad as an actual attack! And then the idea struck me—why not share the sequence that Guruji had given us when we had gone to Kutch? That was a natural disaster and this was a man-made one. I could also share my notes with the students in New York and advise on what we did with the people in Kutch. I quickly sent those notes to Bobby, who was very grateful and told me that she would share them with all the students in the US.

When I was in Pune next, I told Guruji about my conversations with Bobby. He immediately told me that there was a difference between those in Kutch and those in the US. In Kutch, we had gone to a group of people who had no exposure to yoga, and who were in a camp. In the US, the students were already practitioners. They had their own props either at the studio or in their own homes. They could do much more than those in Kutch.

I smiled at my 'dullness'. Why had I not thought of that? It was common sense! But as they say, common sense is not so common. Guruji then gave me the sequence of asanas that could be done in this condition. I shared it with Bobby Clennell, who in turn shared it with the other teachers across the US. The feedback that we got was so satisfying. One teacher said, 'This sequence has been a godsend for the severely traumatised students who narrowly escaped death, and/or who witnessed the event close-up. It is also helping the rest of us who are numb with shock, or just exhausted from it all.'

And one of the students said, 'The sequence of asanas, my teacher said, was meant to help us with the recent events here. Events that have left us grieved and exhausted emotionally, physically, and spiritually. I just wanted to offer my humble thanks to Guruji Iyengar. The sequence demonstrated the amazing strength and power of yoga. It is almost overwhelming to realize this power of yoga to heal. That it is given to us is a great gift for which I am grateful.'

The sceptics asked me how one could expect yoga to help in such conditions. These people needed counselling.

They needed to talk to someone. They needed to get their fears out. My idea then was not to take the place or role of therapists. We needed to help people who were suffering. And if there was a possibility for yoga to heal, why not? The real purpose of yoga is divine and higher aspects of kaivalya, a state of eternal emancipation from the cycles of birth and death. But how can a man who is suffering look in that direction? Why not make an attempt to ease the pain of those suffering?

They still ask, especially those who have never been exposed to yoga: how can asanas and pranayama be of help in such trying times like this disaster? My answer is simple, maybe even simplistic.

Emotional shock and mental tension are immediately reflected in an alteration in our breath. We gasp on seeing a gory sight; we unconsciously hold our breath when faced with tragic news; our heart beats faster as we approach a tense situation... If the mental state is reflected in a disturbed pattern of breathing, why cannot the breath be used as a tool to modulate a disturbed mind? However, when we are in a disturbed state of mind, the breath is also disturbed, and it is difficult to modulate and control. It is here that asanas play a very important role. Specific postures performed in a specific sequence for a specific period of time alter the breath and our state of mind, bringing clarity and emotional stability.

We all hope and pray that we don't experience any such traumatic situation in our lives. But the trauma of losing someone dear is a reality of life. We all have to experience it and live with it. We let time heal us, but the scars sometimes remain, especially if a loved one has departed prematurely or suddenly.

This sequence became very popular across the world as a sequence to withstand and cope with trauma. Therefore I share this with you. For methods to perform these asanas, we can refer to *Light on Yoga*, *Yoga: A Gem for Women*, *Yoga: A Path to Holistic Health*.

List of asanas to cope with trauma

- Shavasana
- Supta Baddha Konasana (with support for the spine)
- Supta Virasana (with support for the spine)
- Prasaritta Padottanasana (with head support)
- Uttanasana (with head support and legs spread apart)
- Adho Mukha Svanasana (with head support)
- Viparita Dandasana Chair (with head support)
- Shirshasana—Viparita Karani
- Setu Bandha Sarvangasana
- Sarvangasana—Viparita Karani
- Pranayama with a very short kumbhaka after the inhalation

As Guruji clearly said, asanas are not prescriptions but descriptions, so here are some hints for teachers on how to progress with this sequence.

- The emotional strength in students needs to be built up and that is what we need to work at.
- Do not make them do standing asanas or backward-bending asanas in this state.
- All asanas (including Shavasana) should be done with the eyes open since they tend to relive the terrible memories when they are asked to close the eyes. They can focus their eyes at any point in front or on the ceiling.
- Ask the students to imagine as if their eyes are located at their temples and ask them to 'open' these eyes.
- Do not insist on a perfect asana in the current situation. What is important is that they do the asana and stay in it as long as they can.
- For any asana (especially supine), ask them to breathe in such a manner that the breath touches the lateral side of the chest during inhalation and to maintain the touch during exhalation.

As much as we hope that nobody should face traumatic situations in their lives, we do know that it is not possible. In the current scenario, this is bound to happen somewhere, sometime and we do hope that this book helps people cope better.

Acknowledgements

I have no words to express my gratitude to my guru, Yogacharya B.K.S. Iyengar, who revived this ancient Indian subject of yoga and made it accessible to the common man. The manner in which he taught has given meaning to the lives of students, and transformed the way we see things.

I have been inspired by all the 'characters' in my stories, and I am grateful to Shirly Ecker, Kuka Shviro, Sara Tawil, Sharon Dawn Taylor, Birgit Andrews, Mark Zambon and Arti Mehta for sharing their personal as well as teaching experiences with me.

I thank *Hareetz* magazine, Israel, for permitting me to use excerpts from the English translation of Aviva Lori's article 'Defying Gravity', about Shirly Ecker, originally published in Hebrew; and Ram Godar for interviewing Mark Zambon.

My sincere thanks to my fellow yoga practitioner, Veun Chin, for her very attractive and eye-catching cover design.

Finally, I am grateful to Deepthi Talwar for motivating me to write this book and for her crisp editing skills, and Westland Publications for publishing it.

I do hope that I am able to touch the hearts of my readers as much as these stories have inspired me.

Printed in Great Britain
by Amazon

60002272R00102